CHALLENGING PROJECTS in STAINED GLASS

CHALLENGING PROJECTS in STAINED GLASS

The Mt. Tom Stained Glass Artisans

ARCO PUBLISHING, INC.
NEW YORK

Published by Arco Publishing, Inc.
215 Park Avenue South, New York, N.Y. 10003

Library of Congress Cataloging in Publication Data

Main entry under title:
Challenging projects in stained glass.

  Includes index.
  1. Glass craft. I. Mt. Tom Stained Glass Artisans.
II. Title: Stained glass.
TT298.C45 1983   748.5'028   82-18437
ISBN 0-668-05985-0 (Reference text)
ISBN 0-668-05581-2 (Paper edition)

Photographs by Gordon Himmelman and Michael Monahan.
Pattern designs and illustrations by Rudy Swol.

Printed in the United States of America

10 9 8 7 6 5 4 3 2

Contents

Acknowledgments   vii
Introduction   ix
1.   Lampshades   1
2.   Blind Soldering   49
3.   Three-Dimensional Projects   78
4.   Bent Glass   119
5.   Restoration and Repair   130
Appendix   158
Glossary   159
Index   161

Acknowledgments

There are some special people we'd like to mention here who have contributed a great deal to our book and our lives, not the least of which has been their friendship:

Rudy Swol, our gifted artist, designer, and for three of us, our mentor. It is not mere flattery nor hyperbole when we say that we could not have written this book without Rudy's talent, encouragement, and professional assistance.

Lisa Wenzel, Anita's daughter and our efficient secretary and model. Lisa relieved us of many of the tedious but most important details connected with our work. Her cheerful willingness to do anything we asked made our time that much more productive.

Duane Cokely, our colleague at Mt. Tom Studio, for his encouragement, advice, loyalty, and solo coverage of many of our classes which freed up much-needed time for our project work and writing.

Peter Lipski, for his Iris pattern and the sharing of his technique, which provided invaluable core material for our discussion of lampshade methodology.

Lorraine Himmelman and June Monahan, Bo's and Mike's wives, respectively, whose loving patience and personal sacrifices allowed us to devote needed time and energy to our books. We owe them both much more than we can repay.

And, our hundreds of stained glass students, who were the inspiration, in one sense, for our writing this book. We hope that it reflects the many things that you taught us over the years.

Introduction

In *Challenging Projects in Stained Glass* we approach the topics less developmentally than we did in *Starting Out in Stained Glass* because we assume that you are more advanced and have more skills than a beginner or novice. (If you would like an introduction to our system or a good refresher, read *Getting Started in Stained Glass*, which outlines basic techniques for cutting, foiling, caming, and soldering.)

Each topic and the projects in this book, however, *are* treated as a "new" venture for you and we provide step-by-step instructions for accomplishing the required stained glass tasks for the projects. In each chapter we discuss the many general aspects and potential applications of each subject. And we provide detailed by-the-numbers projects for you to practice our techniques.

Each activity we outline is an important and interlocking component of your whole project and will, to varying degrees, affect your finished project. That is why we discuss in detail the reasons for doing the things we tell you to do. We try to illustrate and conceptualize our instructions for you, referring to and integrating all the techniques that will help you "see" the overall system and structure of the finished project, thereby understanding both better.

Clearly each chapter's topic is broad enough to command a book-length treatment, and perhaps we will do something about that in the future. But for now, each chapter should put you at ease, remove some of your fears of the unknown, and provide the impetus and guidance for your moving on to bigger stained glass challenges. We hope that our book will give you encouragement and expand your participation in a most creative and totally involving art form.

Inez M. Adamowicz, Gordon D. Himmelman,
Michael Monahan, and *Anita M. Wenzel*
THE MT. TOM STAINED GLASS ARTISANS

CHALLENGING PROJECTS
in
STAINED GLASS

1

Lampshades

Many people believe that lampshades are the most difficult of all stained glass projects, and we tend to agree with them. Inconsistencies with patterns, difficult glass cutting, problems with the transferral of flat glass to curved molds, the need for continual adjustments, difficult and awkward assembly positions, gravitational problems with the solder flow when beading, and the many hours of project time—all contribute to the difficulties and occasional frustrations of constructing a lampshade. It is with lampshades (and our three-dimensional projects, also) that the virtues of patience and fortitude, coupled with precise workmanship, are well rewarded.

The two primary types of lampshades are the flat-paneled and "curved" shades constructed with molds. If you have never attempted a shade before, we strongly suggest that you begin with one of our flat-paneled shades before you attempt our curved Iris shade. There is no teacher like experience, and the flat-paneled shade will introduce you to many of our techniques that can be applied to the more complex and difficult Iris project.

In either case, before you begin, you must prepare yourself mentally for the amount of time it will take to complete a lampshade. We have had students who took as long as three months to complete one shade. Don't be tempted to rush merely to "get it done," or you'll be disappointed with your final product.

Flat-Paneled Shades

We've provided three skirt-panel patterns from which you may choose one for your lampshade. Everyone's taste is different and since the body panel and method is exactly the same we thought you would appreciate the choice. (See Figures 1 (a), (b), (c), and (d).)

PREPARATION

1. The first consideration when making a flat-paneled shade is to decide on the size and hanging location for it. Unlike our Iris shade (or any multipieced rounded shade),

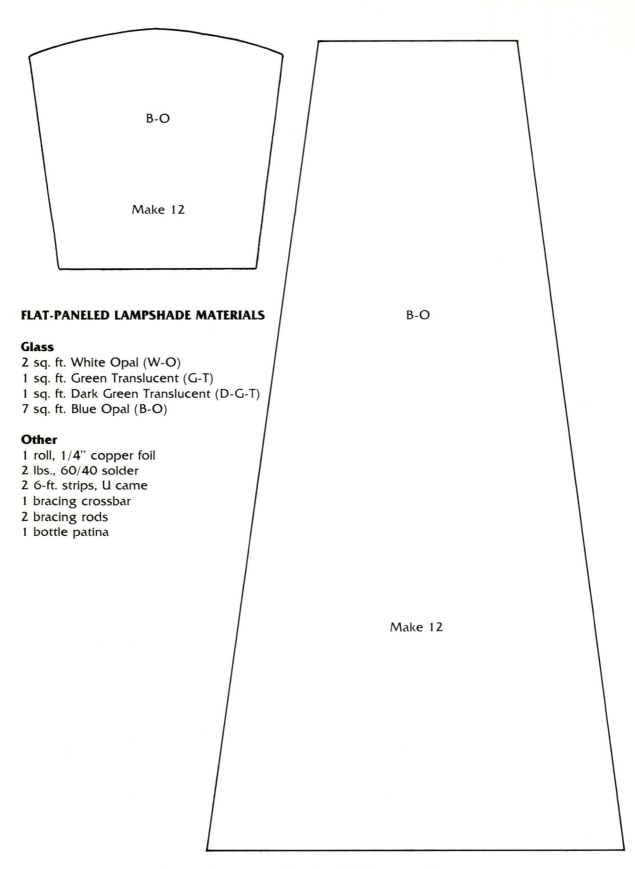

B-O

Make 12

FLAT-PANELED LAMPSHADE MATERIALS

Glass
2 sq. ft. White Opal (W-O)
1 sq. ft. Green Translucent (G-T)
1 sq. ft. Dark Green Translucent (D-G-T)
7 sq. ft. Blue Opal (B-O)

Other
1 roll, 1/4" copper foil
2 lbs., 60/40 solder
2 6-ft. strips, U came
1 bracing crossbar
2 bracing rods
1 bottle patina

B-O

Make 12

Figure 1(a).   Body-Panel and Skirt-Panel Patterns
B-O = Blue Opal

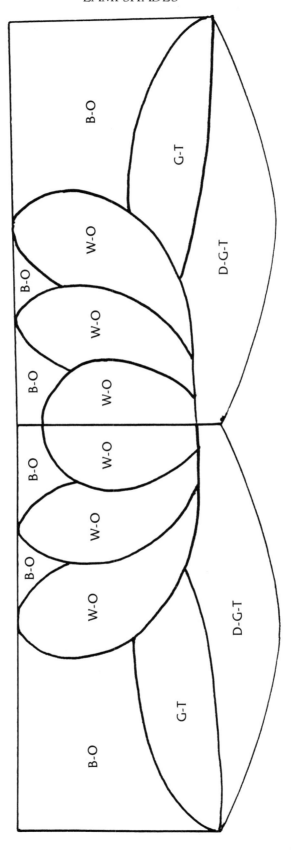

Figure 1(b). Skirt-Panel No. 1
B-O = Blue Opal, W-O = White Opal, G-T = Green Translucent, D-G-T = Dark Green Translucent

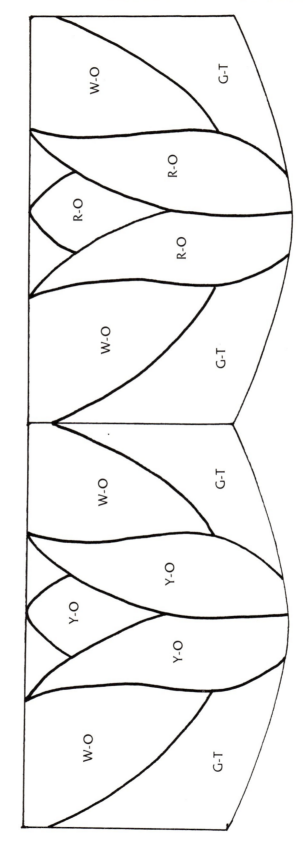

Figure 1(c). Skirt-Panel No. 2
W-O = White Opal, G-T = Green Translucent, Y = Yellow Opal, R = Red Opal

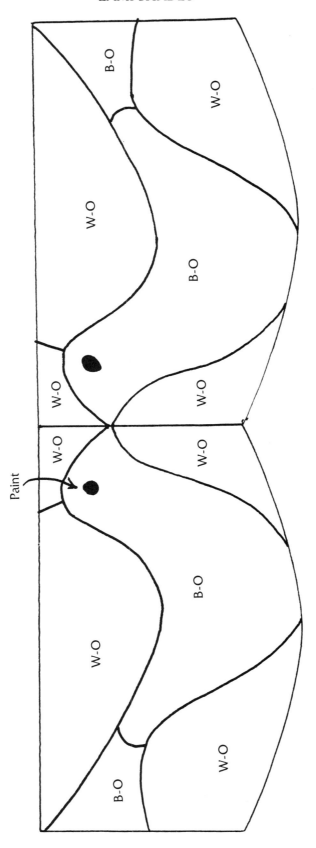

Figure 1(d). Skirt-Panel No. 3.
B-O = Blue Opal, W-O = White Opal

TOOLS AND MATERIALS

Tool/Material	Brand/Description	Available At . . .
FLAT-PANELED SHADE		
Cutting and soldering tools, materials, supplies, and glass in the amounts suggested on the pattern sheets		
Batten strips	1/4″–1/2″ wide	Lumber yard
Plywood soldering board	2′ × 2′	Lumber yard
Plastic pails or buckets	8″ — 12″ diameter	Building or construction supplier/Fish store (for throw-outs)
Push pins	One box, 5/8″ leg, steel point, aluminum head	Art store/ Office supplier
Brass brazing rods	1/16″ or 1/32″	Quality craft supplier
Metal crossbar with universally threaded hole	Varying length	Hardware store/ Stained glass supply
2 Bubble levels	1 short, 1 long	Hardware store
Electrical hardware		Electrical supply
Patina (optional)	**Allnova**	Stained glass supplier

you won't have a styrofoam mold to give you an exact model of its size and shape. That is why you should make a poster-paper mold of our shade to see if the size, shape, and depth is what you want. This will give you an exact replica of the shade provided.

The panel body we present here will give you a shade 13 inches high, 11 inches deep from the bottom of the skirt to the top of the shade proper (excluding the crown), and 16 inches in diameter. The angle of the tapered body, the width of its bottom and top edges, and its length and the height of the skirt and crown panels are, naturally, the determining factors in regard to size.

If you cut out poster-paper templates of the 12 body-panels and 12 skirt-panels and then tape them together at the joints, you'll see the exact size of the shade. If you want to enlarge or shrink the pattern, you can customize the shade for your specific needs.

Besides size factors, predetermining the location is necessary for choosing the correct type and color glass to complement surrounding furniture and room colors. Generally, opalescent glass is the best type since it is opaque enough to hide the bulb and electrical hardware, and yet will diffuse the light for a soft, yet bright, illumination.

BODY-PANEL CUTTING

2. After you've made these very important decisions, and bought the needed materials, you can begin execution. Cut out one copy of our panel pattern on heavy paper.

3. Using a straightedge at both the top and bottom, cut out a strip of glass the exact height of our body-panel (8½ inches), and long enough to accommodate twelve pieces. (You might have to cut two or more strips depending on the size of your sheets of glass. Using the following methods, a strip 40 inches long will yield 12 pieces.)

4. Beginning with *one side only* of your pattern, trace and cut that one side with your straightedge. You should use the straightedge because you especially want the edges free from bumps or indentations since their aligned close butting is extremely important at assembly. (See Illustration 1-1.)

5. If the cut and separation of glass is completed successfully (look below for our NOTE to cover unsuccessful cuts) and accurately, then trace, cut, and separate the other side of this panel. You will wind up with one completely cut-out panel. (See Illustration 1-2.)

Illustration 1-1

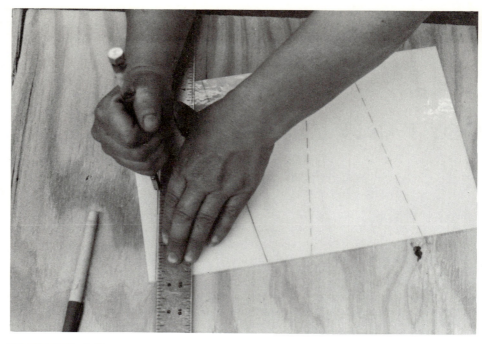

Illustration 1-2

NOTE: When using this cutting method, it's possible to make one of two mistakes: (1) If one cut fractures unevenly and destroys one side of your strip, take your pattern, placing it ¹/₂ inch from the jagged edge, and begin again, or (2) If your panel is larger than your pattern, or you have a few rough spots on your edges, place your pattern on top of this oversized/bumpy panel and trace the correct edge. Then place a strip of masking tape exactly along the mark line. File or router your panel to the edge of the tape and finish with a carborundum stone.

6. Reversing your panel pattern from top to bottom, using the edge of your previous cut as one side, trace the remaining side, cut, and separate your second panel.

7. Continue steps 2 to 6, always tracing and cutting only one side at a time, until you have cut all 12 panels. Then place these panels safely aside.

8. Repeat steps 2 to 7 for the crown pattern.

SKIRT-PANEL CUTTING

1. In order to ensure uniformly exact skirt-panels, you must make a blocking board and frame for them. (See Illustration 1-3.) Take your master pattern and place on a large enough board and construct a four-sided frame around it. *Make sure that the top of this skirt pattern section is perfectly square (90°) and the exact width of the bottom of the body-panel section. (See Illustration 1-4.)* This will be very important when it is time to assemble the various sections. This will also prevent your individual skirt panels from "growing" as you cut out the individual pieces, foil, and put them together.

Illustration 1-3

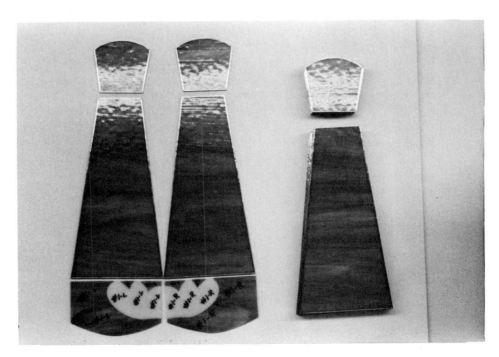

Illustration 1-4

Illustration 1-5

As an additional matching and accuracy safeguard, compare a panel's base with the top of one skirt-panel to make sure they're the same width. This will allow for slight individual panel deviations and, in effect, guarantee a custom skirt for each panel. Then number the corresponding pieces after you have finished with each skirt panel.

2. Cut out and foil each piece of glass.

3. *Taking care not to touch any of the edges, including the top and bottom,* solder the skirt-panel on both sides, stopping ⅛ inch from the edges on all the foiled seams, and raising a nicely rounded, finished bead.

4. Repeat steps 2 and 3 for every skirt-panel, using the same master-pattern blocking board and frame.

5. After all your skirt panels are soldered, foil the body- and crown-panels which you cut out previously. (See Illustration 1-5.)

ASSEMBLY

Now that you have finished soldering all the skirt-panels and foiled all the body- and crown-panels, clean off the worktable. You will need to complete the assembly process at one sitting, so don't begin unless you can devote enough time to accomplish a secure assembly. Place everything within easy reach—all your panels, flux, flux brush, solder, heated iron, a pencil and marker, push pins, rubber-tipped hammer, and a large plywood soldering board at least 2' × 2'.

Illustration 1-6

It would also be a great help if you had someone to provide an extra set of hands when assembling the shade. But, since in many cases there will be no one available, the following technique will allow you to assemble the lampshade on your own:

1. Pick up a body-panel in each hand and place the bottoms flat and straight up on your soldering board with the inside bottom points (corners) touching each other.

2. Tilt the tops of each panel inward and down toward your soldering board until they meet, never allowing the bottom edges to leave the soldering board.

3. Position your hands so that the left is holding the pair at the top at the butting edge, and your right hand is at the bottom. *For all the next steps, always keep your left hand on the panels.* (Since the world is right-handed, you left-handed people should probably reverse these and any other hand positions we mention.)

4. With your right hand, tack two pushpins in your board one inch in from both edges of your left panel, and tack two other pushpins at either edge of your right panel. These four pins will create a support base that you can push against as a third hand which will prevent the panels from slipping when you tack-solder them. (See Illustration 1-6.)

Illustration 1-7

5. With your right hand, flux the center foil seam 3 inches from both the top and bottom. (See Illustration 1-7.)

6. Still holding the pair with your left hand, pick up your soldering iron with your right, melt some solder on your tip, and transfer it to the fluxed areas. Make sure no solder gets near the top or bottom of your section because it will interfere with your skirt and crown assembly. (See Illustration 1-8.)

7. Slowly and carefully rotate your tacked pair of panels to the left so that you have room in front of you to add the next panel.

8. Install two more pushpins in the same position to support your original first panel.

9. Pick up another panel (still holding the tacked section with your left hand) and place it against the right side of the tacked section, tilting it downward to match the angle of its butting panel.

10. Move your left hand over to support the new panel and pinch it at the top to line it up with the tacked pair.

Illustration 1-8

11. Flux and tack-solder this third panel to the other two in the same manner as steps 5 and 6. (See Illustration 1-9.)

12. Repeat steps 7 through 11 for the rest of the panels. You will be continually rotating the tacked-panel sections to the left, adding pushpins to the original first panel for foundation support, holding the growing tacked section with your left hand, while adding new panels and tack-soldering with your right. (See Illustration 1-10.)

13. After all the panels are initially tack-soldered, add one-inch globs along the seams for extra strength. *Once again, do not get any solder along the edges.* Do not worry about neat soldering beads now, because we will take care of that technique later. Right now we are only interested in strengthening the section so it will not come apart while we are handling it during the rest of the assembly process. (See Illustration 1-11.)

14. Place your well-tacked body section upside-down into the pail mentioned on the Tools and Materials list (page 6) and generously solder the inside seams. The bucket will keep the rounded shape of the panel section as you go around. (See Illustration 1-12.)

Illustration 1-9

SKIRT ASSEMBLY

1. After completely soldering the inside of the body-panel section, you will begin to attach your skirt sections *while the body section remains upside down in the pail.* Take the first two skirt-panels in either hand and align them with the bottoms of the two corresponding body-panels. Tilt them inward, pinching them at the top until they match and join. (See Illustrations 1-13 and 1-14.)

2. Holding the left section steady and stationary (see Illustration 1-15), remove the right skirt section and flux and tack-solder the left section to the body-panel in two places with your free hand. (See Illustration 1-16.)

3. Pick up that second skirt section that you removed and pinch it and the tack-soldered skirt section together at the bottom and tack-solder it to the adjoining panel-body section first and then to the skirt section. (See Illustration 1-17.)

4. Continue repeating steps 2 and 3 around the circumference of the lamp, always moving to the right and matching up the correct panel/skirt pairs, *never taking your supporting left hand away from the tacked sections.*

Illustration 1-10

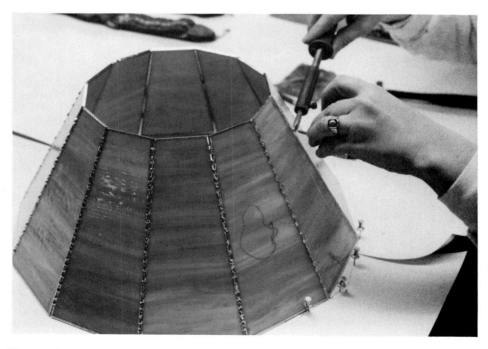

Illustration 1-11

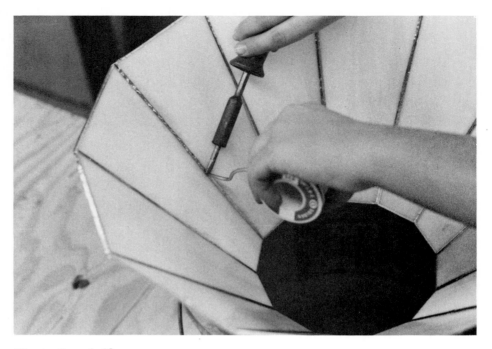

Illustration 1-12

Illustration 1-13

Illustration 1-14

Illustration 1-15

Illustration 1-16

Illustration 1-17

If, when you get to the last skirt section, it does not fit properly, trace a custom pattern, build a new blocking frame, and recut and install any new pieces you will need in the skirt. You do not want to force a too large skirt section into the gap, which will create stress problems with the other sections, nor do you want a section that is too small and will create a loose skirt bonding and large and unattractive solder seams after the gaps are filled.

5. After all skirt sections are tack-soldered, do some additional tack-soldering on the inside seams as well as outside, using the one-inch glob method, spaced intermittently.

6. When the lamp is securely tack-soldered and unwavering, take the lamp out of your bucket with both hands and forearms on either side, and stand it right-side up on your table.

SOLDERING

1. Now that the lampshade is securely assembled, you need to finish the soldering with neat, smooth flowing, rounded beads. The trick is to use gravity to your advantage rather than allow it to be a hindrance. The solder will flow best if you prop the lamp in some way in order to make level the seam(s) you are soldering.

2. Starting with the inside seams first, prop the shade under the outside surface, and on the opposite side of the seam you are going to solder, prop it by using rags or crumpled-up newspaper or paper toweling. You will not have too much trouble leveling the lamp since it will lie flat on the worktable for the body and the butting skirt/body seam.

3. However, in order to solder the outside seams, you will need a bucket or cardboard box large enough in which to place the lampshade. (see Illustration 1-18.) You will also need a small line level. (a) Place the lampshade inside the pail or box and prop the lamp with newspaper until one of the panel seams appears level. Make sure that one skirt-panel does not totally support the weight of the lamp. Your newspaper, properly placed, should relieve the pressure. (b) Place your level on the seam and adjust and prop the shade until the bubble is level. (See Illustration 1-19.) (c) Then flux and solder the seam. (d) Repeat this procedure—propping, leveling, fluxing, and soldering—all the way round the panels for all the foiled seams.

CROWN

1. After the inside and outside seams are soldered to your satisfaction, place the lamp right-side up back on your worktable.

2. Take two crown sections and place them directly on top of the body panels at the aperture. Now set up and tack-solder the crown exactly as you did the skirt-panels, steps 1 through 7, pages 11 and 12. (See Illustration 1—20.)

3. After tack-soldering the outside and inside seams, you will have to prop up the lamp in order to get a smooth-finished bead, but be careful not to prop it at such an angle that one of the skirt or crown sections will crack.

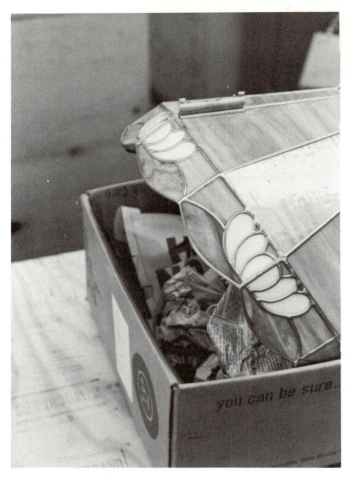

Illustration 1-18

BRACING

Probably the main reason that many lampshades begin coming apart and even crash down (a common problem) is that their apertures and crossbar, the points from which the lampshade will hang, and which will support its full weight, are not properly reinforced. We have solved this problem by bracing the lamp in the following manner:

1. Cut off two 12-inch pieces of your brass brazing rod.

2. Take one and measure 5 inches up from the bottom and bend it with your pliers to form an L-shaped rod.

3. Measure the top of one of the body-panels and mark the same length on the longer section.

4. At that marked point, bend the longer side to create a U-shaped rod in a shape to conform to the tapered seams of your body-panels.

5. Bend and shape the second brazing rod to match the first one.

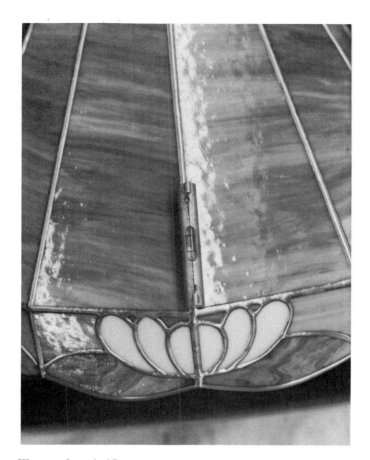

Illustration 1-19

Illustration 1-20

Illustration 1-21

6. Flux and tin (solder) both rods all over to prepare them for overlaying them into the lamp's seams.

7. Strip (remove all the solder) the four solder seams that will receive the brazing rods. Choose any two panels *opposite* to one another.

8. Turn the lamp upside down in the bucket or cardboard box, prop it, and set one brazing rod into a seam by fluxing and tack-soldering at the top, middle, and bottom. (See Illustration 1-21.)

9. Repeat step 7, soldering the other rod in a seam exactly opposite to the first one.

10. *Except for the top horizontal edge,* completely and generously solder both brazing rods into the lamp seams. You should have a slightly raised and rounded bead that will hardly be noticeable.

CROSSBAR

In order to accurately pinpoint the center of your crossbar so that your lampshade will hang evenly, proceed in the following manner:

1. Turn your lampshade upside down.

2. Taking a strip of paper as wide as your crossbar but *longer* than the diameter of your aperture, measure exactly, and mark on the paper the distance between the glass

Illustration 1-22

of the panel with one brazing rod and the other glass/brazing rod panel. (Do not stop short of the glass and measure just to the solder on the brazing rod.)

3. Cut off the excess paper.

4. Fold your paper in half.

5. Place the paper with the folded crease exactly in the middle of the hole in the crossbar.

6. Mark both ends of your strip on the crossbar.

7. With a hacksaw, cut off the excess metal. You should now have a crossbar that has been customized for your lamp.

8. Tin the edges of your crossbar about 2 inches toward the center on both sides. If the solder will not "take," file and scrape away any finish until the silver metal shows through.

9. Now center the crossbar on your brazing rods with the hole directly in the middle of the aperture. (See Illustrations 1-22 and 1-23.) If you do not center your hole, the lampshade will hang at an uneven tilt.

10. Solder well the tinned crossbar to your brazing rods on both sides, the top and bottom, turning the lamp over when needed. (See Illustration 1-24.)

Illustration 1-23

FINISHING TOUCHES

In order to provide a finished border to the crown and skirt, we suggest wrapping each with a heavy U came. This is why we kept telling you not to solder the edges. This will give the lampshade a little more substance and body while reinforcing the entire lamp. And it will be a much stronger material which will resist fraying, as the soldered foil might do. Procedure:

1. Your copper foiled edges should still be unsoldered. Remove all the foil with a razorblade, taking care not to cut away any vertical foil that touches the outer edge.
2. Stretch out a piece of came that will completely encircle the edge of each skirt-panel.
3. Begin wrapping your skirt by soldering one end to a butting skirt seam. (See Illustration 1-25.)

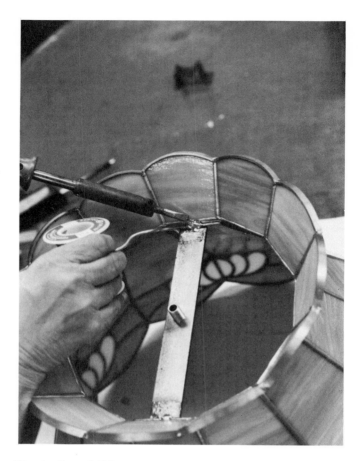

Illustration 1-24

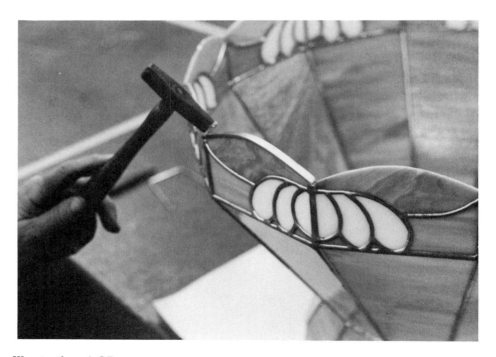

Illustration 1-25

4. Continue wrapping along one skirt-panel to the next vertical butting seam, making certain that the glass is tightly set into the came. Then flux and solder the came to the vertical seam. (See Illustration 1-26.)
5. Continue around the entire skirt, doing one skirt-panel at a time, tapping the came tightly in place before you solder.
6. After the skirt is completely wrapped, solder every adjoining seam in the skirt-panels to the lead came. This will create a strong bond for the came and prevent its coming apart from the skirt.
7. Repeat all the previous steps with the crown. (See Illustration 1-27.)

Now that this is completed finish off the lamp:

1. Scrutinize the soldered seams for wrinkled or dappled areas, especially at the crossroads sections. Vigorously rub these areas with 000-extra-fine steelwool. This will smooth out your beads in these areas.
2. Thoroughly wash the entire lampshade with a warm water and ammonia solution and glass cleaner.
3. And, finally, if you prefer, patina your soldered seams with any one of the commercially available patinas (e.g., Allnova products) to turn the solder a dark black or copper shade. Finish by polishing with Glass Wax®, Brasso®, or a silver polish. (See Illustration 1-28.)

Congratulations! You've just gone through a stained glass "baptism-of-fire" that few people will experience. What you've just accomplished, in essence, is the creation of not just a lamp, but a family heirloom. All that should remain to do now is to electrify the lamp for hanging. There are various electrical hardware sets, fixtures, and decorative chains you can buy to suit your taste and needs. Most hardware stores or electrical supply outlets will be glad to provide all you'll need; and some may even show you how or actually put them together for you. Make certain you bring your lamp along when you go, to ensure a custom fit.

The Iris Lampshade

Before you attempt a lampshade of this complexity, we would hope that you have acquired expert cutting skills and have completed some other flat-paneled lamps, since a molded lampshade will challenge every one of your stained glass skills as well as try your patience. Our intricate pattern will require a time commitment unlike any other. But, when complete, you'll have a lamp second-to-none.

PREPARATION

There are four important areas in the preparation stage for constructing a rounded or shaped lampshade: (1) designing your pattern; (2) choosing your glass (and color);

Illustration 1-26

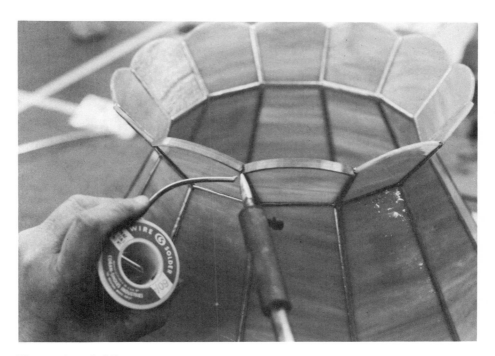

Illustration 1-27

Illustration 1-28

(3) selecting or making a mold; and (4) the transferral of the design from the paper to the mold or vice-versa. We've provided the design and glass information for you in this chapter; we'll now discuss in detail steps for areas 3 and 4.

THE MOLD

There are various molds made from different materials available from stained glass suppliers. You can buy "whole" molds that will give you an exact idea of the size and shape of your finished lampshade; or you can buy a section mold (as we did for the Iris), which will require repeated uses to complete the required number of lamp sections. You can also purchase all six sections and glue them together to form the "whole" mold. Or you can always make your own mold from scratch, using materials like styrofoam or ceiling insulation.

For the Iris shade we chose a Worden, 6-repeat, C-20 mold with a rounded upper body. (If you buy a "blank" mold, you won't have to paint over the design.) We altered its shape slightly to create a deeper lampshade by enlarging it in the following manner.*

1. We glued a block of styrofoam, approximately 6 inches thick and exceeding the edge, to the bottom. This will add the depth we wanted.

2. After the glue set overnight, we took a serrated bread knife and shaved off the excess styrofoam to conform to and continue the contour of the mold.

3. We then overlaid the butting styrofoam seams with Spackle (a pasty white joint compound), using a putty knife, blending it into the gap, and evenly smoothing it over to match the surface of both. Allow about six hours for it to dry to a relatively hard finish.

4. You should now sand down the joints until they are as perfectly shaped to the contour of the original mold as possible.

5. With a flat, white latex paint, coat the entire section two or three times. This will give you a "blank" mold upon which you can transfer your design.

6. From a piece of cardboard,** cut two varying-width vertical borders that are contoured to fit both edges. Permanently attach them (with Elmer's glue) to the sides, raising them above the edges (creating a "lip") to prevent and block any glass from overlapping the mold. This border will give you a perfectly straight panel edge that will ensure that your butting sections will line up correctly and fit tightly.

You should now have a custom-shaped, blank mold section that is ready for the design you need to draw on the mold in order to have a true and accurate reference point for your glass cutting.

DESIGN TRANSFERRAL

The process of transferring our design from the paper patterns to the mold will take painstaking accuracy, many adjustments, and constant alteration. You *must* be as precise and exact in this process as possible since this mold design is your prototype for the entire lampshade:

1. Begin with your vertical bordering sections (Pattern 1; Figure 2 (a)). Make a copy of each of the patterns, cut them out, place them on your mold, and trace their outline on either side.

2. Take your cloth tape and measure the exact center of the panel section (top and bottom) and draw a straight line down the center to the bottom of the mold. This dividing line will be your main point of reference for the rest of your pattern-transferral process.

---

*The following technique outlines a method for customizing a standard mold or even making one from scratch. You do not necessarily have to do this if you choose a mold that will accept our design.

**This cardboard is included in the Worden mold package.

3. Next, transfer the top 6 rows of the design (Pattern 2; Figure 2 (a)). The important point of this horizontal section (and the entire gridwork of the lampshade), when you are ready for cutting, is that your band of pieces be the exact width.

So, to help guide you in this area, hold your cloth tape at the top left of the mold and mark and divide each horizontal row (1–6) of pattern 2 according to the given widths as they descend.

4. Transfer the tape to your center line and mark and divide each horizontal again.

5. Shift the tape to the right section of the mold and repeat the same procedure. You should now have three reference points through which you can draw free hand *with a pencil* the slightly curved horizontal gridwork of the top third of the lamp. When this is completed, you will have the borders and the horizontal lines on your mold.

Don't be too discouraged if our patterns do not line up exactly with your measuring points. That is par for the course. You'll have to adjust our patterns to your mold all the way through this transferral procedure.

6. Now cut out in *one piece* the inner portion (the diamond and the curved pieces attached to it and the adjoining descending pieces) of the pattern and line up the tip of the diamond on your center line. Then while fanning the paper out, trace the outline of this internal section. You should now have completely drawn the top third section of the panel section.

7. Now transfer the bottom rows (13–15) and scalloped border (pattern A; Figure 2 (c)), lining it up with your vertical borders and center line.

8. Next take the left-center gridwork (rows 7–12, pattern 3; Figure 2 (b)) and transfer this to your mold in the same manner as steps 1 through 4. These rows should be easier to transfer since they are all of equal width and you already have two other sections and center line as guides.

9. Transfer the right-center gridwork (pattern 3) as you did with the left center gridwork in step 8.

10. Next, place the Iris itself on the mold (pattern 5; Figure 2 (d)) with the right tip of the flower touching the center line and common line between rows 6 and 7, with the stem lining up as closely with the stem pattern in the bottom bordering section. The tips of the left and right leaves should terminate exactly at a horizontal line. (Ours terminated at the bottom [left leaf] and the top [right leaf] of row 9.)

After the outline is transferred, cut up the Iris flower paper pattern into individual pieces and trace them on your mold, *one-at-a-time. Place the cut-outs aside (in a box) and save for your glass cutting.*

Finish the Iris leaves by continuing the horizontal row lines through the appropriate areas on the leaf pattern.

11. Now that you have completely transferred the entire lampshade pattern to the mold, you must make custom cutting-patterns *not from our given patterns* but from the pattern designs on your mold, because you probably had to alter our flat patterns in order to transfer them to the mold. (See Illustration 1-29.)

As you trace, cut, and put aside each pattern, number at the edges both the mold pattern and the cut-out patterns. By numbering each pattern at the border, the number will not be pulled away by the two-way tape that you will eventually place on the back of the glass; and the numbering will make it easier to identify the cut pieces and its corresponding place on the mold.

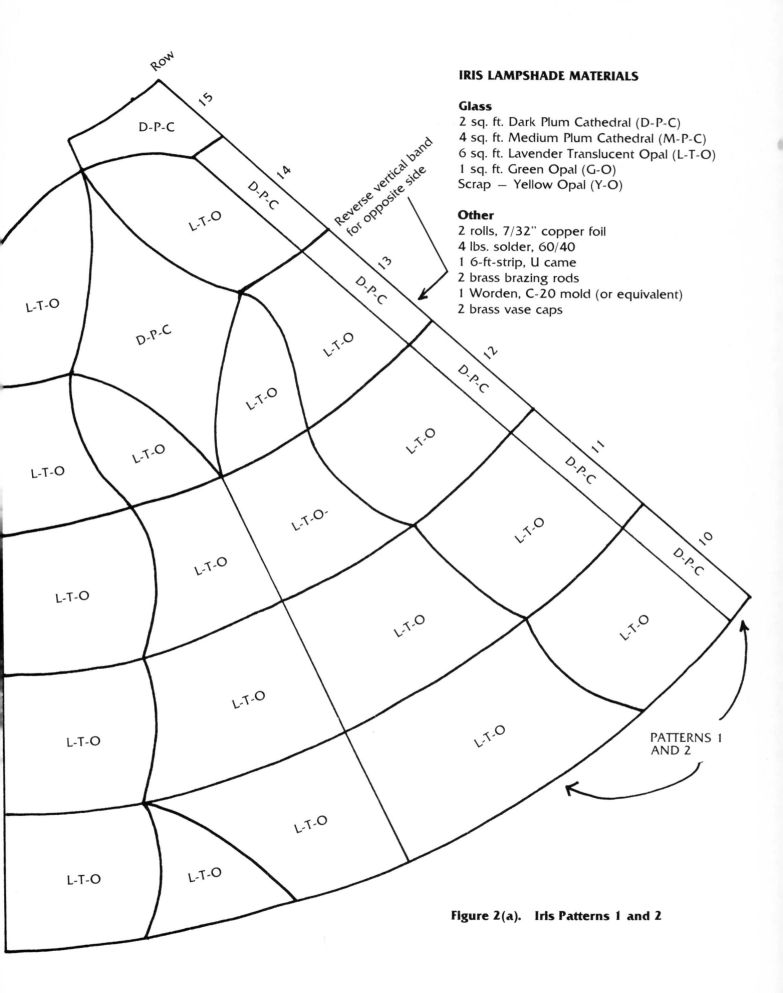

IRIS LAMPSHADE MATERIALS

Glass
2 sq. ft. Dark Plum Cathedral (D-P-C)
4 sq. ft. Medium Plum Cathedral (M-P-C)
6 sq. ft. Lavender Translucent Opal (L-T-O)
1 sq. ft. Green Opal (G-O)
Scrap — Yellow Opal (Y-O)

Other
2 rolls, 7/32" copper foil
4 lbs. solder, 60/40
1 6-ft-strip, U came
2 brass brazing rods
1 Worden, C-20 mold (or equivalent)
2 brass vase caps

Figure 2(a). Iris Patterns 1 and 2

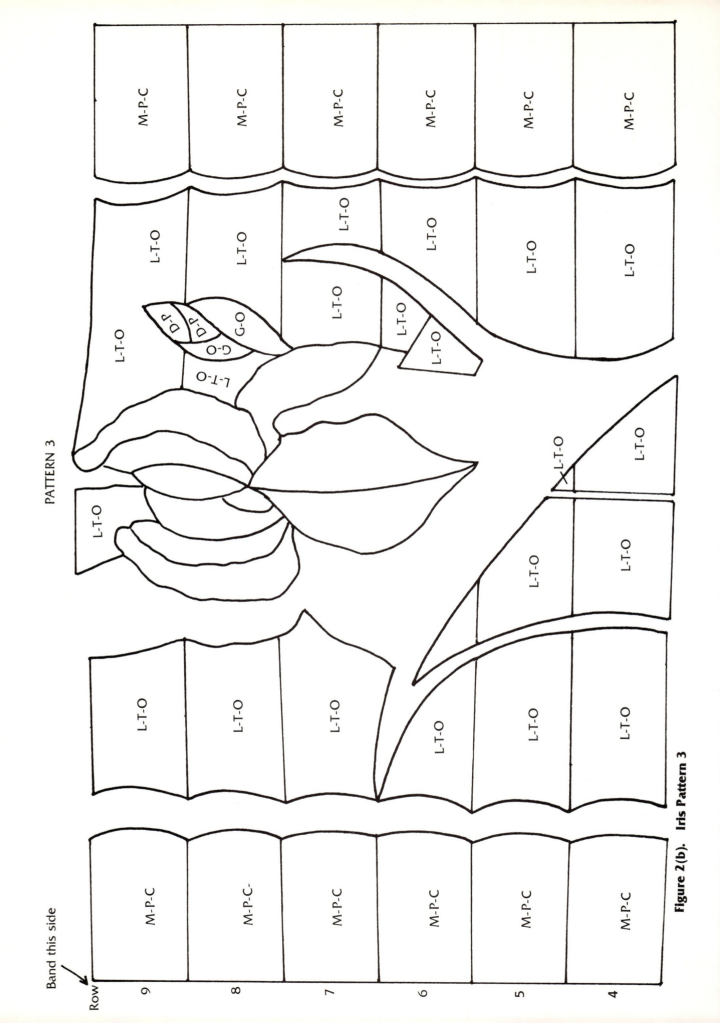

PATTERN 3

Band this side

Row

Figure 2(b). Iris Pattern 3

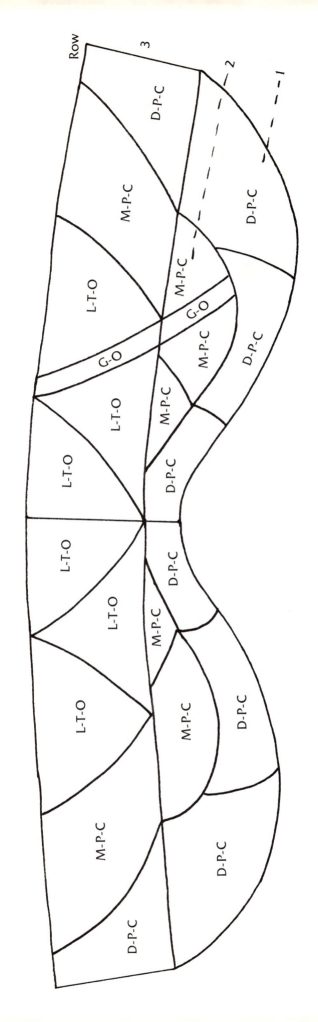

Figure 2(c). Iris Pattern 4

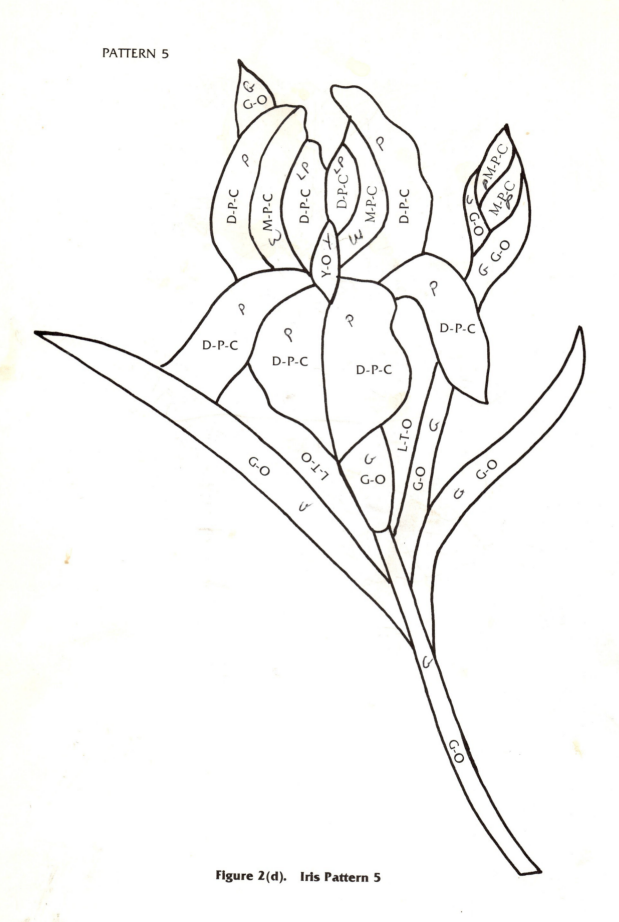

Figure 2(d). Iris Pattern 5

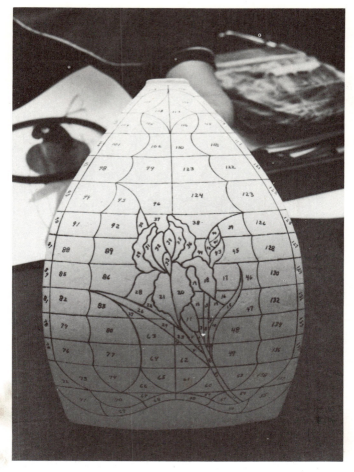

Illustration 1-29

Now that your mold and design are prepared for the glass, you can move on to the execution. But before you begin, make sure your pattern is exact and as perfect as it can be. It is the only guide you'll have for assembling the lamp; and if it is "off" anywhere, it will be a cumulative mistake that will have negative consequences when it is time to put everything together.

CUTTING AND FITTING

1. Begin your cutting with the bottom border pieces first. Cut a long strip of glass slightly larger than the width of one border piece. You can then cut individual border pieces of all the same width from this one long piece. This border outline must be as uniform as possible because a viewer's eye is most likely to notice any deviation in it as opposed to any internal ones. (See Illustration 1-30.)

2. As you cut each piece, place it on the mold using the thicker hatpins to support it. You will *never* remove these hatpins as you go from section to section

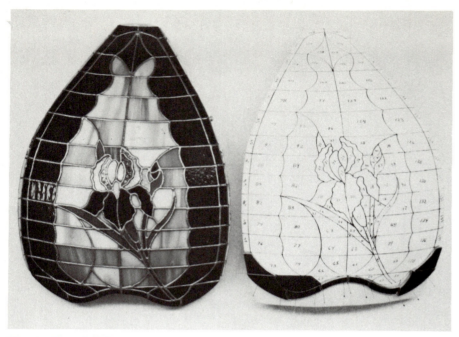

Illustration 1-30

because they are your bottom support and guide for the lamp and a uniform border. Make sure you can see your ink outline all around the piece. (This will allow space for the foil.)

3. You will then place an extra-small square of two-way tape on the back center of the piece and place it back on the mold. This two-way tape will help the glass adhere to the mold and prevent the glass from slipping. (You can stop taping the glass to the mold after you pass the rounded hump and the glass lies flat on the mold.)

4. Outline each taped piece with the thin common pins, *making sure that the pins tightly butt and push against the glass.* These pins will allow space for the minute width of the foil (that will accumulate when you wrap each piece) and prevent the section from "growing" because of the foil. You won't remove these pins until you foil each piece later. (See Illustrations 1-31 and 1-32.)

IMPORTANT: Never, with a molded lamp, cut all your pieces at once before you compare each one to your mold pattern. You are cutting flat pieces of glass from a flat pattern and then attaching them to a curved surface. *It will take constant cutting adjustments as you go along because of this physical paradox.* Although it might not seem it, it really is easier and less frustrating in the long run to cut every pattern piece by piece and then place them on the mold than to cut many pieces and then try to place them all on at once.

5. Now, cut and pin row 14 (patterns 1 & 2; Figure 2 (a)) in the same manner as steps 1–4, once again. *Make sure you can see the ink outline on the mold pattern of each piece of glass when it is taped to the mold, so you will have a spot in which to stick your pins.*

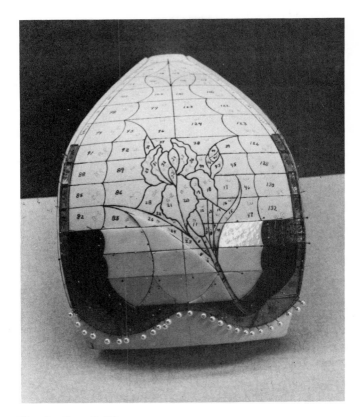

Illustration 1-31

6. Now begin to cut row 13, proceeding from the left border to the center. Insert pins all around to reserve space for the foil. Stop at the center and proceed from the right border to the center. As mentioned in step 1, you can alter center pieces slightly and the eye will not detect minor deviations. But since the border outlines are more geometric and exact, this method will ensure exact borders. Remember to do the center portions last.

7. Continue cutting and pinning rows 11 and 12 and then stop! You should have the first five rows from the bottom cut out and pinned. (See Illustration 1-33.)

You're now ready for foiling and tack-soldering:

FOILING AND TACK-SOLDERING

We should mention before you begin foiling that you should be extremely careful with your intricately or deeply curved pieces. The foil will have a tendency to split, especially on the inside curves. You should slowly stretch it out little by little, working it down and around the edges. If the foil does split you should either rewrap or overlay a small piece of foil to cover the crack. The solder will adhere only to the foil, not the glass; if you do not patch the split foil, the finished seams will have numerous random

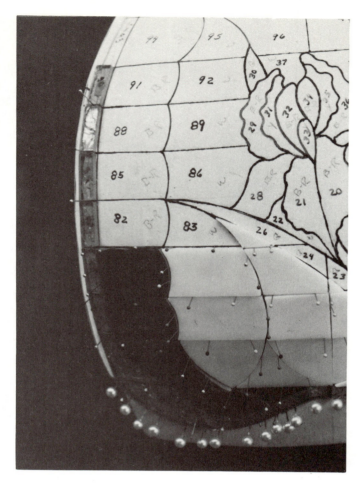

Illustration 1-32

gaps in the soldered seam and distract the viewer's eye. Taking care of this detail is one of those important minor techniques that eventually becomes a major characteristic of your work and distinguishes the quality craftsmanship from the mediocre.

Okay, let's begin:

1. Start your foiling with the bottom border, removing the common pins separating the foiled pieces from their abutting pieces as you replace each foiled piece. (*Remember:* Do not remove the hatpins because these are supporting all the pieces.) As you replace each foiled piece, make sure it snugly butts the adjoining piece(s). *But don't press the foiled piece too hard against the mold* because you might have a difficult time removing the completed section from the mold when it is time to remove the entire section and begin another. (See Illustrations 1-34 and 1-35.)

    Incidentally, you can stop taping the glass after the first seven or eight rows are completed when you should be over the hump of the mold and your glass is no longer vertical but lying flat on the mold.

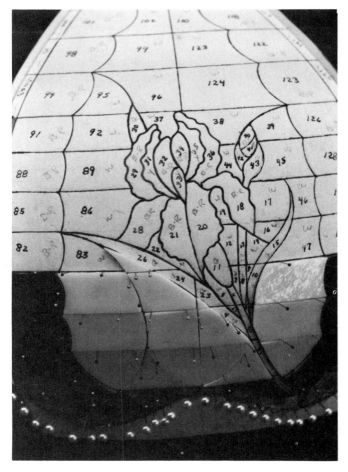

Illustration 1-33

2. *Foil the first four rows and leave the fifth row unfoiled.* (We will tell you why later.)

3. *Prepare the first three rows only* for tack-soldering by lightly fluxing all the joints where four pieces of glass come together at the corners and on the horizontal joints where two pieces come together. Don't flux any of the foiled edges or any foil other than the first three rows. (We will tell you why later.)

4. Tack-solder all the fluxed joints, taking care not to hit any of the edges because a wayward glob of solder will be an obstruction to the sections butting together tightly when it is time to assemble all six. (See Illustration 1-36.)

Your mold should now have five rows of glass on it, the first three rows of which are foiled and tack-soldered, the fourth row that is only foiled, and the fifth row that is unfoiled. The last two rows are unsoldered or unfoiled because the foil, and especially the solder, acts as a weight or cushion against the glass. The glass will have a tendency to "pick up" at the points that are not soldered. You don't want that fourth or fifth row to pick up and raise the contour of the lamp away from the mold.

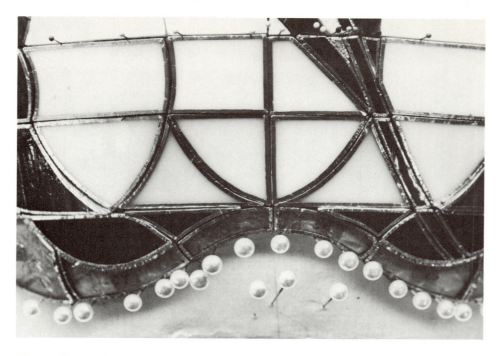

Illustration 1-34

Illustration 1-35

Illustration 1-36

There is one very important point to make at this stage: Most people's intentions when they begin a lamp are honorable: that is, they are ready for the challenge, motivated and intend to do the project quickly. But other commitments sometimes prevent their finishing the shade as fast as they initially intended.

The problem with copper foil is that, if allowed to remain exposed to the air for any great length of time, it will oxidize and tarnish, and a green film/mold will coat the foil, especially if there is any excess flux present after tack-soldering. This tarnishing will make soldering a nice, rounded, finished bead impossible because the solder will not adhere to the altered state of the foil.

A good technique for preserving the foil's natural bright finish, if the foiled section is to remain idle for more than a month, is to cover the foiled section with plastic wrap. Or you can cover the entire mold with a large plastic garbage bag and tuck it under the mold to keep air out. Either of these precautions will retard the corroding of the foil and facilitate the final soldering, whether you are able to do it within a relatively short period of time or not.

Also, to avoid getting stale, take occasional long breaks from doing the lamp when you feel yourself getting tired or impatient to finish.

5. As you complete each row, in order to ensure that each completed panel's horizontal row will line up with each other when it is time to assemble them, mark with a ballpoint pen the exact center of the foiled horizontal rows on the bordering cardboard edge all the way up to the top. (See Illustration 1-37.)
6. Continue all the way up to the top—cutting five rows, wrapping four rows, and tack-soldering three rows. (See Illustration 1-38.)

Illustration 1-37

SOLDERING

After the entire lampshade section is wrapped and tack-soldered you must naturally finish soldering a rounded bead on the outside *and* inside. This is a crucial process and must *not* be rushed:

1. You will first have to gingerly remove the entire section from the mold, taking your time because the panel section has a tendency to stretch and expand and place stress on the foil which will pull it apart.

Without removing the bordering hatpins, using a thin putty knife (or a similar tool) slowly pry and lift the lower section (the first seven or eight rows you taped) from the mold. *Do not force the glass from the mold* because you will damage your foil and mold if you are too aggressive.

2. Remove the two-way tape from the back of the glass and gently place it in a box stuffed with crumpled newspaper while you perform the next step.

3. Place a strip of thin aluminum foil over the mold and press it down flat. This foil will protect your mold and extend its life (for use with other lampshade patterns), since it will shield any errant solder that drops off your foil from burning holes in your mold.

Illustration 1-38

4. Carefully pick your section up and place it back on the mold, pressing it down so it conforms as closely as possible to the contour of the mold.

5. Begin at the top, fluxing and soldering smaller sections at one sitting (4–5 rows), using the leveling and propping methods as outlined in the Flat-Panel Section, p. 19. You'll find that soldering this molded section will be more difficult, more tedious and more time consuming than with the flat-paneled lamp, so be prepared to take your time. *Remember: Don't solder or flux the outside edge of the vertical bordering strips nor the bottom border.* These edges will be taken care of at assembly time. (See Illustrations 1-39 and 1-40.)

6. After doing your best job on the outside of your lamp, remove the panel, place it upside down in your cardboard box, and finish soldering the inside. Do an equally good job on the inside as you did on the outside. People cannot resist looking inside a lamp, and if it is half-heartedly flat-soldered, it will only detract from the rest of your good work.

7. As a finishing step, thoroughly clean the entire section. Take care not to damage the unsoldered foiled edges, especially the right and left borders that will butt the other adjoining panels. (See Illustration 1-41.)

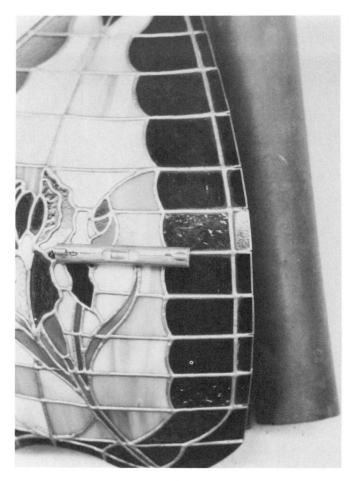

Illustration 1-39

Wipe and dry and place the finished panel in a large plastic trashbag. Place it aside in a safe place until all six sections are completed. Now that you have completely finished one panel, you have to repeat all the previous steps in order to make five more finished sections. Ready . . . begin!

ASSEMBLY

All done? So soon? That was quicker than we thought. Now it's time to sum up all your parts and make an even greater whole!

1. Enlist the aid of a willing soul with steady hands and a brave heart to help you. *Do not attempt to put this shade together yourself.*

2. Inspect the unsoldered foiled edges for mold, tarnish, or tears. If it is torn, you'll have to replace it. If any foil is tarnished, gently rub it with the fine steel wool to

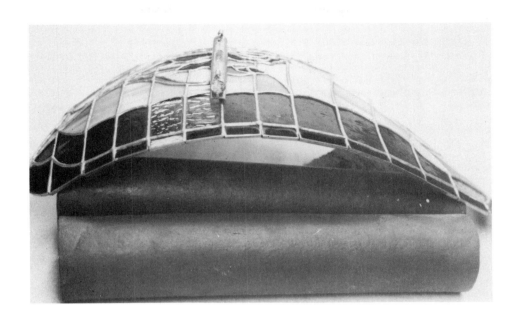

Illustration 1-40

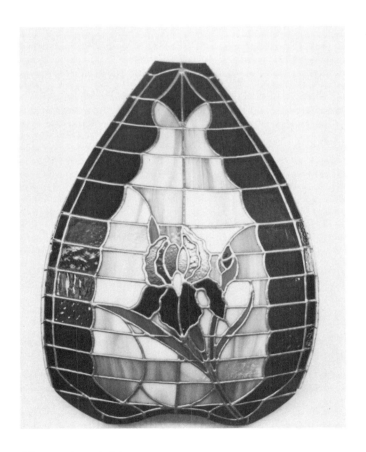

Illustration 1-41

remove it or else the solder will not adhere to it.

3. With small amounts of solder, tack-solder two of the sections together, lining up the horizontal rows so they match as closely as possible. You may have to try different combination pairs of panels to get the best matching pair, but it is imperative that you start off right. (If nothing matches and the butting edges are too far "off" you'll have to remove some pieces, recut custom pieces, and insert the new pieces.)

4. Tack-solder the remaining sections to the assembled sections, adding one section at a time to the assembled sections, in the same manner as you did for the flat-paneled body (pp. 10–13). If a section does not line up by butting it on one side of the tacked section, try lining it up with the opposite side of the same section. In other words, try different pairing combinations for exact horizontal matches as you proceed in the assembly.

5. If your final section does not line up or fit properly into the last gap, heat (with your soldering iron) the inside vertical bordering seam of the uncooperative section and press gently until it conforms and meets the rest of the lamp.

6. When the entire lamp is together, tack-solder the butting seams with 1-inch globs of solder at the bottom (*don't hit the bottom border*), middle, and top of these connecting seams.

7. Carefully place the lamp upside down in a large bucket and tack-solder the inside seams.

8. Remove it from the pail, put it back on the form (or some people lay it on its side, using newspaper for a cushion), and finish soldering your "good" bead. Do the same for the inside seams, following the leveling method until all the connecting seams, inside and out, are as uniformly soldered as all the other seams.

It is important to note here that in the shifting, lifting, and soldering of the sections, an occasional piece of glass might break or crack. Unless you want the cracks in order to reflect a reproduced antiquity, replace any fractured pieces following our method outlined in the Restoration chapter, p. 130. Their presence will only gnaw at your artistic pride for the life of the shade.

BRACING

In order to handle and strengthen your lampshade, you will need to solder a double vase cap to your aperture. This is an alternate bracing method to our brazing rod technique that can be used with multipiece shades.

1. Measure the diameter of your aperture and purchase 2 vase caps (at an electrical supply or hardware store), one of them $1/2$ inch larger and the other $1/4$ inch larger than the diameter.

2. (a) If you are going to patina your lampshade seams, and also wish to do so with your brass vase cap, you will have to tin (solder over) the brass because brass will not accept patina. (If you don't want to patina the brass, skip this step and move on to step 3.) Flux the entire *outside of the larger vase cap* and slowly begin soldering smaller sections of it, building up the large amount of heat that you will need in order for the brass to

accept the solder. Only be concerned here with building up layers of solder. Do not worry about a smooth finish yet; coverage is what you are after.

(b) After building up the solder, pick it up with pliers (*because it will be hot!*) at the top, tilt it, and apply slow heat again, proceeding from the top to the lip, allowing the excess solder to run off. Make the solder coating as smooth as possible.

3. Place the smaller vase cap inside the lamp, with the hole at the top, and the larger vase cap on the outside, resting on top of the lamp in the same position as the inner vase cap. (See Figure 3.)

4. Insert a 4-inch electrical nipple through both vase caps with a nut at both ends. Tighten the nuts with your fingers, lining up both vase caps evenly over the aperture so that the nipple is in the center of the aperture and your vase caps are centered on the glass.

5. Flux and tack-solder the *outside* vase cap to every intersecting solder seam.

6. Turn your lamp upside down in a bucket and tack-solder the inside vase cap to the intersecting seams. Your lampshade is now braced and prepared to accept the electrical hardware for hanging.

FINISHING TOUCHES

1. You should now wrap that unsoldered, bottom edge with lead came according to the procedure outlined in the Flat-Paneled section, pp. 24–26. This will give your lamp a finished, sturdy edge that will not disintegrate as the foil might have done.

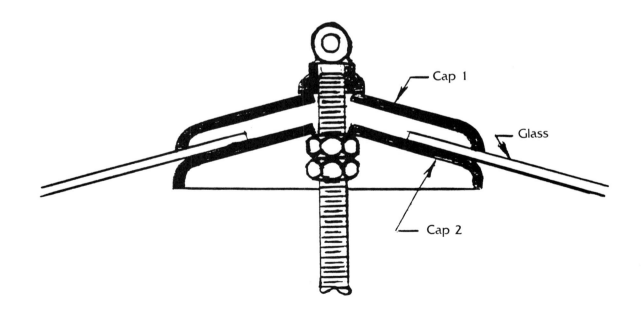

Figure 3.

2. If you have a tub large enough in which to place the lampshade, lay a towel for protection on the bottom, and gently wash the entire lamp in warm water and soap. Use a hard-bristled toothbrush, but do not apply excess pressure because you may crack some glass that is under any stress.

3. If you want to "antique" the shade with patina, apply it with a soft cloth, and then polish it (if you wish) with Brasso, silver polish, or copper polish.

4. As with the flat-paneled shade, bring your shade to an electrical supply store in order to acquire the necessary parts to electrify it.

Summing Up

Well, this was quite a chapter, wasn't it? If you accomplished all the tasks and finished both of our lampshades, you can be proud of yourself. Your fortitude and patience produced two family treasures that will become priceless as the years go by.

Before you head into any of our other chapters, take a long break to appreciate what you have done and savor the knowledge that you have accomplished something few people can do. You will also need this time to get those creative juices flowing again that will carry you to the other stained glass projects that follow.

2.

Blind Soldering

Blind soldering is our term for a process by which one piece of glass can be securely mounted on top of another piece without gluing or soldering it on the face of the project. The applied glass is anchored by means of a brass pin which is passed through a precisely drilled hole and then soldered on the back of the host glass. The glass crafter is drilling holes "blind" in the sense that every hole must be planned and preset; and the soldered joint cannot be seen by the viewer; the viewer is "blind" in regard to the joint—hence, the name.

There are many applications for this technique: instead of overlaying glass at an edge, in order to solder it to an existing joint, you can now securely place glass pieces directly in the middle of a project, or anywhere else, for that matter. Jewelry boxes, mirrors, three-dimensional objects, panels—anything—can now accept other glass to create reliefs, add depth, and improve utility. You do not have to sacrifice design or decorative aspects because of what heretofore was physically impossible to accomplish.

Tools and Materials

Styrofoam or Heavy Cardboard Sheet.   By placing the glass to be drilled on top of either of these materials, it will prevent your drill bit from going through the glass and whatever work table underneath.

Brass Rods.   Brass pins are attached to the glass you are mounting, passed through the host glass, and then soldered to its backside. The brass will "take" the solder better than steel pins and you do not have to worry about their rusting if any stray moisture from the drilling gets on them.

¼-Inch Electric Drill.   A hand-held drill will work but requires extreme care and patience. If you have a drill press, it will be better.

Router.   The Glastar router with a flexible shaft and diamond bits is a far superior tool for drilling than the hand-held drill. It is faster, more accurate, and there is less chance of your shattering the glass or mirror.

Carbide and Diamond Bits.   Carbide bits work fine and are relatively inexpensive. We will discuss diamond bits later on in the chapter. (See Illustrations 2-1 and 2-2.)

49

TOOLS AND MATERIALS

Tool/Material	Brand/Description	Available At . . .
Styrofoam or heavy cardboard sheets	1 1/2" sheets/blocks	Construction supply
Kerosene	4–6 oz.	Hardware store
Needlenose pliers	Offset at 90° angle	Hardware store
Eyedropper		Drugstore
Heavy paper	Six 8" × 10" sheets	Stationery store
Wire cutters/dykes	Standard or heavy size	Hardware store
Brass brazing or welding rods	1/32" diameter	Welding supply or quality craft supplier
Variable-speed drill or drill press		Hardware store
or . . .		
Router and flexible shaft	**Glastar**	Stained glass supplier
Various carbide or diamond bits (for router)	1/32" and 1/16"	Hardware or glass store
Glazing compound or putty	1 can **Dap**	Hardware, paint, or glass supplier
Soldering tools		
Conical (pointed) soldering tip	**Standard, Esico**	Stained glass supplier

Kerosene.   This will be the lubricant for reducing friction when drilling.

Glazing Compound or Putty.   This creates a dam for forming a lubricating pool for the kerosene when drilling.

Methods

Before getting into any specific projects and detailed techniques, we should stress one very important factor: *Drilling holes through glass is a delicate and time-consuming operation.* Glass is not like a piece of wood where you squeeze the trigger of your drill,

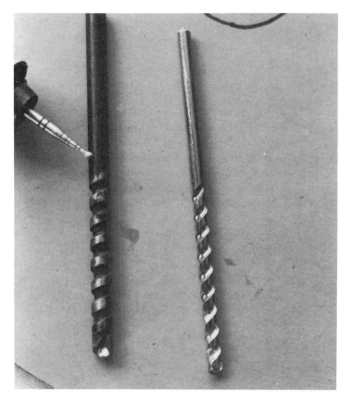

Illustration 2-1

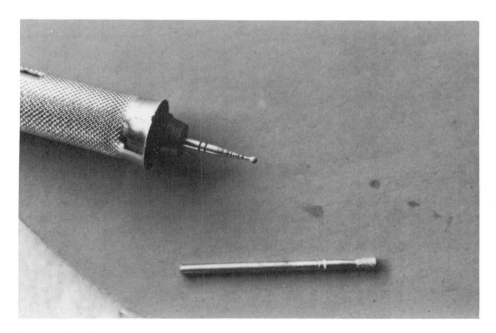

Illustration 2-2

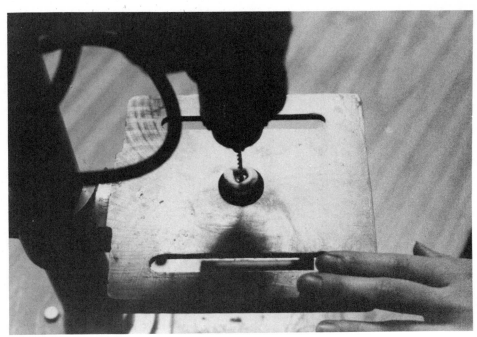

Illustration 2-3

press hard, and Zammo! you're through quickly. Contrary to its fragile nature, glass is a very hard substance to drill completely through. Sometimes it takes 15 to 20 minutes to properly drill one hole through a piece of glass 1/16-inch thick. As in all other stained glass endeavors, patience is the key to blind soldering.

Before attempting a "live" project, you should practice drilling holes through regular windowglass. Get your drilling tools and materials, and some windowglass, and proceed as follows:

1. Place your styrofoam or cardboard sheet on top of your work table. Place your windowglass on top of that and, with a felt-tipped marker, mark a spot to be drilled near the center of the glass.

2. Roll out a string of putty about the length and diameter of an unsharpened pencil.

3. Make a circular dam around your work by pressing the putty to the glass. The enclosure should create a "pool" area about the size of a quarter. (See Illustration 2-3.)

4. Fill up your putty dam with kerosene in order to lubricate the bit and glass, which will get hot while drilling.

5. Just as your father admonished you to let your handsaw do all the work rather than your arm, let the drill now do your drilling. *Do not press the drill into the glass. The slightest bit of excess pressure will fracture the glass.* Just the weight of the drill itself should be applied to the glass. Start your drilling by steadying the drill with one hand and *lightly* coming down on top of the glass until the bit makes a slight impression on your drill work. (See Illustration 2-4.)

6. After you start the drilling, wobble the top of the drill very, very slightly in a circular motion. We find that this slight wiggle seems to make the drill penetrate a

Illustration 2-4

little faster and better than letting it stand perfectly steady. Remember: *Do not rush this.* It may take anywhere from 5 to 20 minutes to make this hole. And . . .

7. *Do not drill through the other side of the glass.* When you see that the bit is starting to penetrate through the bottom of the glass, the kerosene should siphon off. The minute this happens, *stop drilling!*

8. Turn your glass over, and with an eyedropper, apply some kerosene to the almost-punched-out hole. (See Illustration 2-5.)

9. Very gently, finish drilling the hole from this backside. If you continued on through from your original side (especially with a mirror) there is a good chance you would fracture the glass. The reservoir of kerosene that seeped into the hole will eliminate the high risk of fracture.

Drill several more practice holes until you feel that you know what you are doing. Do not worry if you fracture some pieces along the way; everyone does initially and it is the only way you will develop a feel and technique for the drilling.

Now, you can do all your drilling for blind soldering and our projects with your variable-speed drill (or drill press) and your carbide bit. But, for those of you who wish to go to the expense, diamond bits will work faster with less chance of glass breaking. If you use or purchase a Glastar router, an optional flexible grinding shaft is available with a set of diamond bits. The diamond bits cut drilling time and the flexible shaft fits right in your hand like a dentist's drill. The method is relatively the same as with carbide bits, with a few exceptions.

1. Set up your glass on top of the styrofoam.
2. Mark a spot to drill and carefully begin drilling your hole, making just a slight indentation in the glass.

Illustration 2-5

3. Stop drilling and with your eyedropper drop *water (not kerosene)* into and around it. *If you don't lubricate with water, you'll ruin your diamonds.*
4. Continue drilling, *making sure you occasionally add water as needed,* gently rotating the shaft of the drill while pivoting the bit, just as you would with a carbide bit and variable-speed drill.
5. As you are about to break through the bottom, the sound of the drilling will be different. When you notice this "lighter" sound, ease up on the pressure and you will be able to go right through without turning or damaging the glass.

Those of you who elect to use diamond bits will find the drilling much faster and easier. And you will have the option of purchasing sets of bits that will give you many more drilling possibilities than with carbides. However, as mentioned previously, this expense is an important consideration.

With either type of bit, we would like to emphasize, once again, that patience is the virtue that will ensure success. Practice drilling multiple holes varying distances from one another with regular windowglass until you yourself know how long it will take to drill them and what the reaction of the glass will be. After that, try our first project.

Projects

The Butterfly Mirror

This is a good introductory project that will bring you step-by-step through our entire process and get you ready for tackling our Mt. Tom Train or any other larger project. (See Figure 4.)

First a few preliminary steps:

1. Cut out a mirror 9½ inches in diameter.
2. Cut out and assemble your butterfly. However, *on the bottom side of your butterfly (which is going to lay flat against the mirror) flat-solder it. Do not build up a rounded, rolling bead.* This will enable the butterfly to lie flat on the mirror. Whenever you mount glass on top of another piece, remember to always flat-solder the back of the top piece so it will lay flat against the bottom or host piece.
3. Cut out an exact paper pattern (using heavy paper) of the mirror that you will use as a semi-template for drilling. You will always need to cut out a paper template for any host glass for any project to ensure proper drilling. (See Illustration 2-6.)

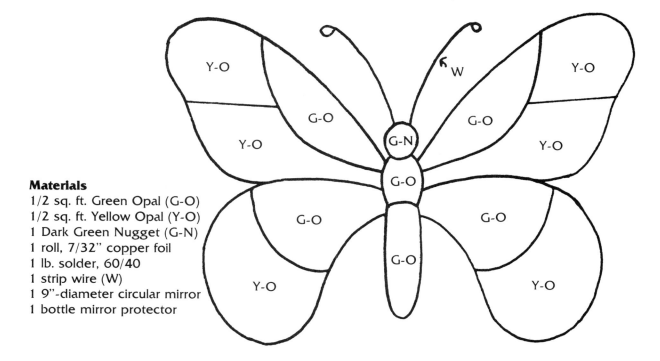

Materials
1/2 sq. ft. Green Opal (G-O)
1/2 sq. ft. Yellow Opal (Y-O)
1 Dark Green Nugget (G-N)
1 roll, 7/32" copper foil
1 lb. solder, 60/40
1 strip wire (W)
1 9"-diameter circular mirror
1 bottle mirror protector

Figure 4.   Butterfly Mirror

Illustration 2-6

Now, gather all your drilling and soldering tools and materials to begin the actual process:

1. Lay the glass butterfly on the paper template in the exact position that you want it applied on to the mirror. (See Illustration 2-7.)

2. Trace the outline of the butterfly on to the paper and put the paper and mirror aside. (See Illustration 2-8.)

3. Take two brass pins ($^1/_2$ inch long) and tin (solder) them by fluxing and putting a light coat of solder all over them. This will allow the butterfly and mirror to accept the pin more easily without getting the solder and glass so hot that it will fracture the glass.

4. On the back side of your butterfly (the flat-soldered side), mark exactly where you want the pins soldered. Two pins in the center of either wing should be enough to securely anchor the butterfly on to the mirror. When performing this step with other projects, you will have to determine where and how many pins to solder. Usually it is a matter of balance and the size and weight of your project that are the determining factors.

5. With your back side of the butterfly face up, pick up your pins with your needlenose pliers and solder them to your marked points. (See Illustration 2-9.) *Don't build up globs of solder at the pin/butterfly joints.* This is where the conical-point tip is extremely useful. (See Illustration 2-10.)

6. Place your paper mirror pattern on top of your styrofoam or cardboard.

7. With your thumbs over the soldered pins and looking straight downward, line up the butterfly with the traced pattern. Wiggle the pins *through* the paper and

Illustration 2-7

Illustration 2-8

Illustration 2-9

Illustration 2-10

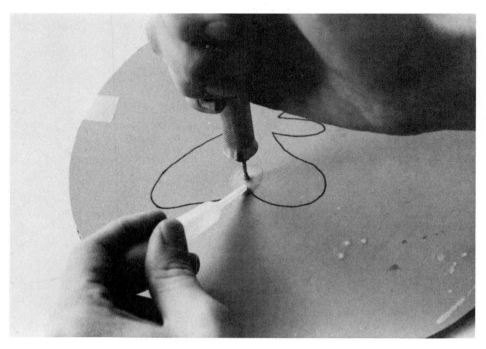

Illustration 2-11

into the styrofoam. This procedure produces our template for drilling.

8. Tape the paper template to your mirror.

9. Then, using the smallest bit you have, put a drop of kerosene (carbide) or water (diamond) into the paper hole before you begin. Drill *slight indentations* into the mirror through your two paper holes. *Do not go all the way through.* (See Illustration 2-11.)

10. After the indentation, take the paper template off and continue drilling on through. For *carbide* bits, build up your kerosene putty reservoir. For diamond bits, make sure you lubricate with water. (See Illustration 2-12.)

11. Insert your pinned butterfly in the holes to make sure everything fits well. If it does not line up, you can adjust your pin(s). If everything is okay. . .

12. Wash your butterfly and mirror well.

13. Replace your butterfly on top of your mirror, which is on top of your styrofoam or cardboard. Your pins should go right through the styrofoam. Press the butterfly tightly enough to the mirror so that there is no rocking motion and it is as tightly pressed to the mirror as possible.

14. With masking tape, secure the butterfly to the mirror so it won't move or fall off when you turn the mirror over in step 15.

15. Turn the mirror and butterfly over and lay it flat on your worktable. Coat the back of the mirror and all holes with Glass Pro Silver Protector so that the solder and flux will not corrode the mirror's backing. (See Illustration 2-13.) Let dry per manufacturer's instructions.

16. Take a 2-inch strip of ¼-inch foil and with a small nail poke a hole through the center of the strip. (See Illustration 2-14.)

17. Slide it down over one pin until it touches the mirror.

Illustration 2-12

Illustration 2-13

18. Cut off ³/₄ inch of foil on both ends of the strip so that only about ¹/₂ inch remains on the mirror and pin. Strip off the backing and press the foil on to the mirror. (See Illustration 2-15.)

19. Repeat steps 16–19 to the other pin.

20. Flux your pin near the hole. With your 90° needlenose pliers, pull up the pin to ensure that you are tightening the butterfly to the mirror. (See Illustration 2-16.) With your other hand, put some solder on your tip and solder the pin to the back of the mirror, spreading the solder on the foil. Do this to both pins. (See Illustration 2-17.)

21. Cut off the excess protruding piece of brass rod at the solder mound. (See Illustration 2-18.)

What we've essentially done here is anchor the butterfly to a ¹/₂-inch bolt (rod) of solder based on the opposite side of a ¹/₁₆-inch hole. This will ensure that your butterfly will stay stationary for the life of the project. (See Illustration 2-19.)

Finish your project by thoroughly cleaning it, darkening it if you wish, framing or adding hooks and a decorative chain.

Try doing a few smaller projects—attach flowers to jewelry boxes, reliefs, initials to coats of arms, birds to planters, etc., gradually building up your drilling and soldering skill—before you try the Mt. Tom Train.

Illustration 2-14

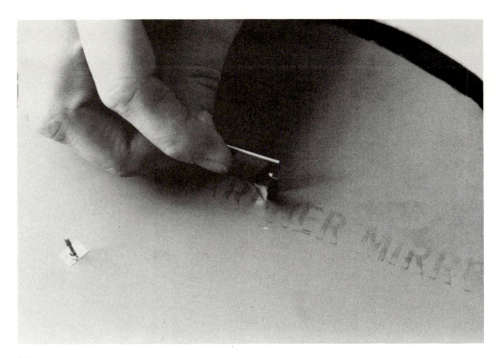

Illustration 2-15

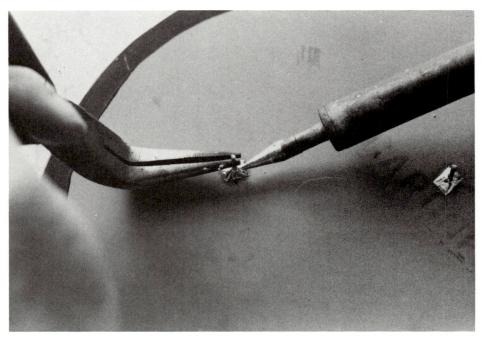

Illustration 2-16

Illustration 2-17

Illustration 2-18

Illustration 2-19

The Mt. Tom Train Mirror

Our Mt. Tom Train is a perfect enhancement for any youngster's bedroom or railroad aficionado's den. But it is not an easy project to accomplish; next to our Iris lampshade, it requires the most time and artistic accuracy of any project in the book. The 75 mirror holes and the 120 railroad ties will dictate a meticulous and patient approach with each piece of glass and individual procedure. (See Figures 5 (a) through (f).)

While most of the steps are exactly the same as the Butterfly project (although many more holes and glass are involved), we will repeat the procedure here and individualize and amplify the procedure where needed.

1. Cut out, foil, and solder all your train pieces. Cut out and wrap your railroad ties and mirror (you'll solder these later). (See Illustration 2-20.) *Remember:* When you solder each railroad tie, flat-solder the backs so they will lie as flat as possible on your host mirror. Also, mark each point where a brass pin will be soldered: each puff of smoke should have 2, the engine 5, the train cars 4, the caboose 2, and each nugget 1. (See Illustration 2-21.)

2. Make your cardboard template of the mirror (to guide your drilling). Lay out your railroad train and nuggets (wheels) in any position you want, and trace the outline of each railroad car. (See Illustration 2-22.) Lay out all your railroad ties and mark a drilling hole on the template for every third tie. After you finish, cut out a rounded corner of the template and place it aside to act as a guide later when you are laying down the came railroad track. (See Illustration 2-23.)

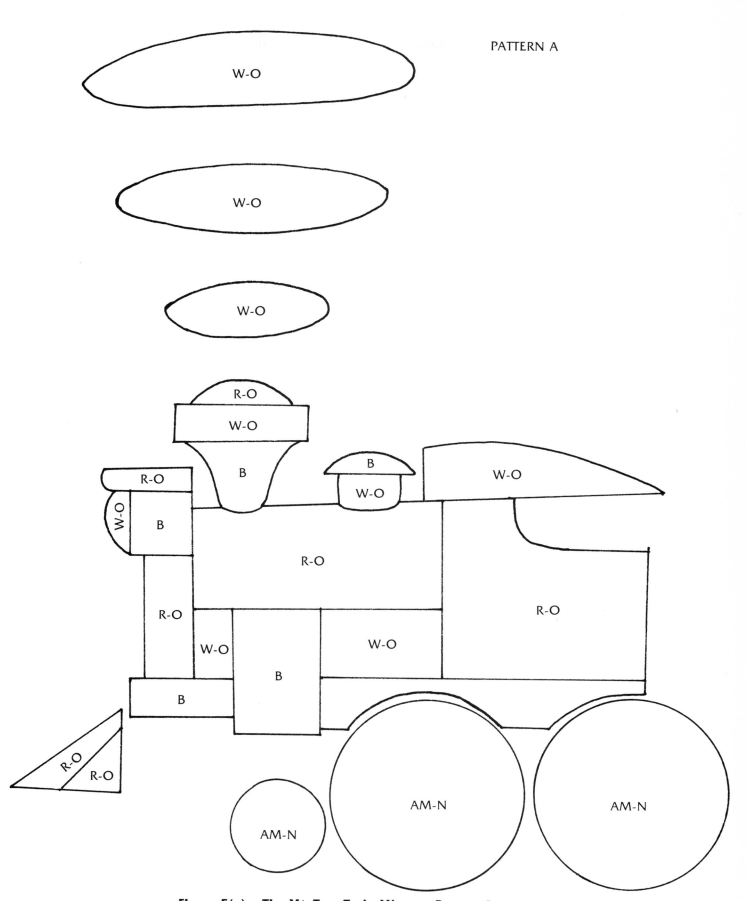

PATTERN A

Figure 5(a). The Mt. Tom Train Mirror — Pattern A

PATTERN B

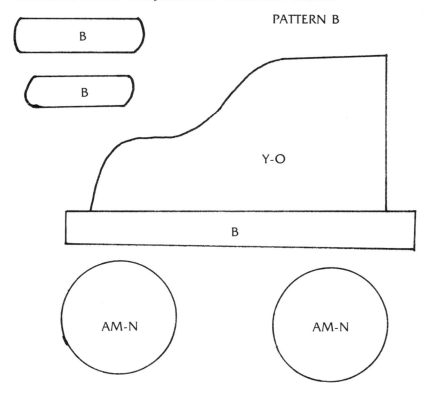

Figure 5(b).   Pattern B

Illustration 2-20

PATTERN C

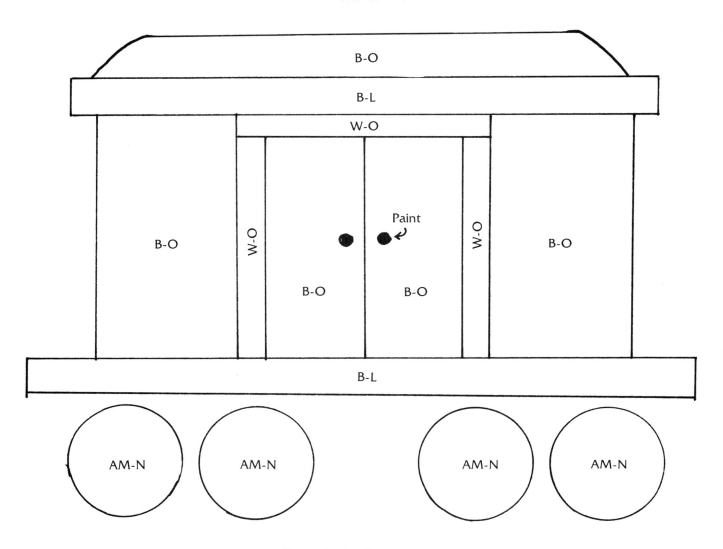

Figure 5(c). Pattern C

3. Tin and solder your ¹/₂-inch brass pins to each car, puff of smoke, and every third railroad tie (you'll attach your brass pins to the nuggets during the drilling process). (See Illustration 2-24.)

4. With your cardboard or styrofoam under your template, line up each piece of glass with its outline and push each individual piece's brass pins through the template. (See Illustration 2-25.)

5. Now for the drilling process. For this large project you should use the Glastar flexible shaft drill and diamond bits, adding a drop of water as you slowly drill each hole. The diamond bits are faster, easier and there is less chance of breakage. (See Illustration 2-26.)

PATTERN D

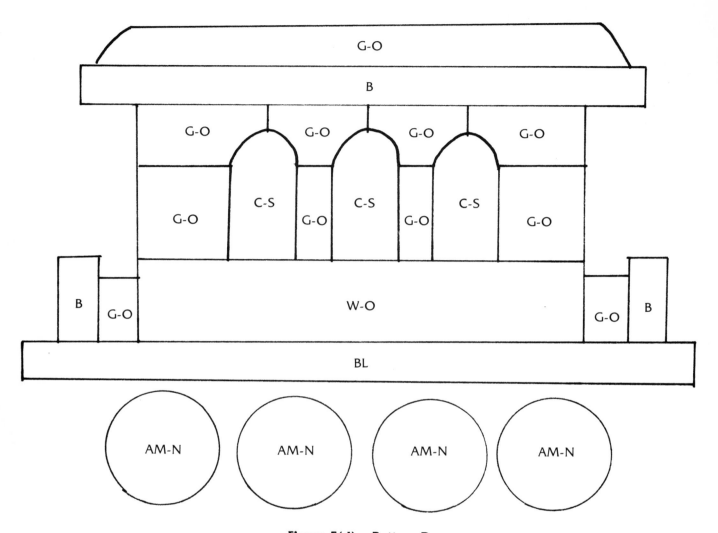

Figure 5(d). Pattern D

Tape your template on top of the mirror and mark each hole on the mirror. Remember to proceed slowly and cautiously; you do not want to crack your mirror at the 70th hole and waste all the previous work.

Your wheels are unique in the sense that you have no foil to anchor the pin. After drilling the hole in the center, overlay a small piece of foil over the foil which should protrude slightly from the front of each nugget. Shape the foil into a circle with your razor and solder the foil and over the tip of the pin so that the solder resembles a hubcap on the wheel.

After all the holes are drilled, *make sure you thoroughly clean your mirror to prevent corrosion.*

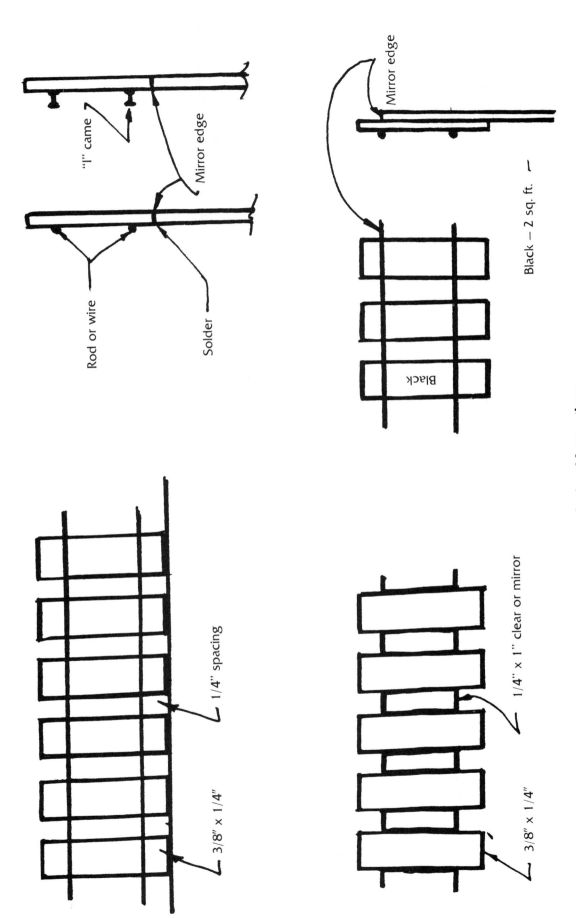

Figure 5(e). Optional Instructions

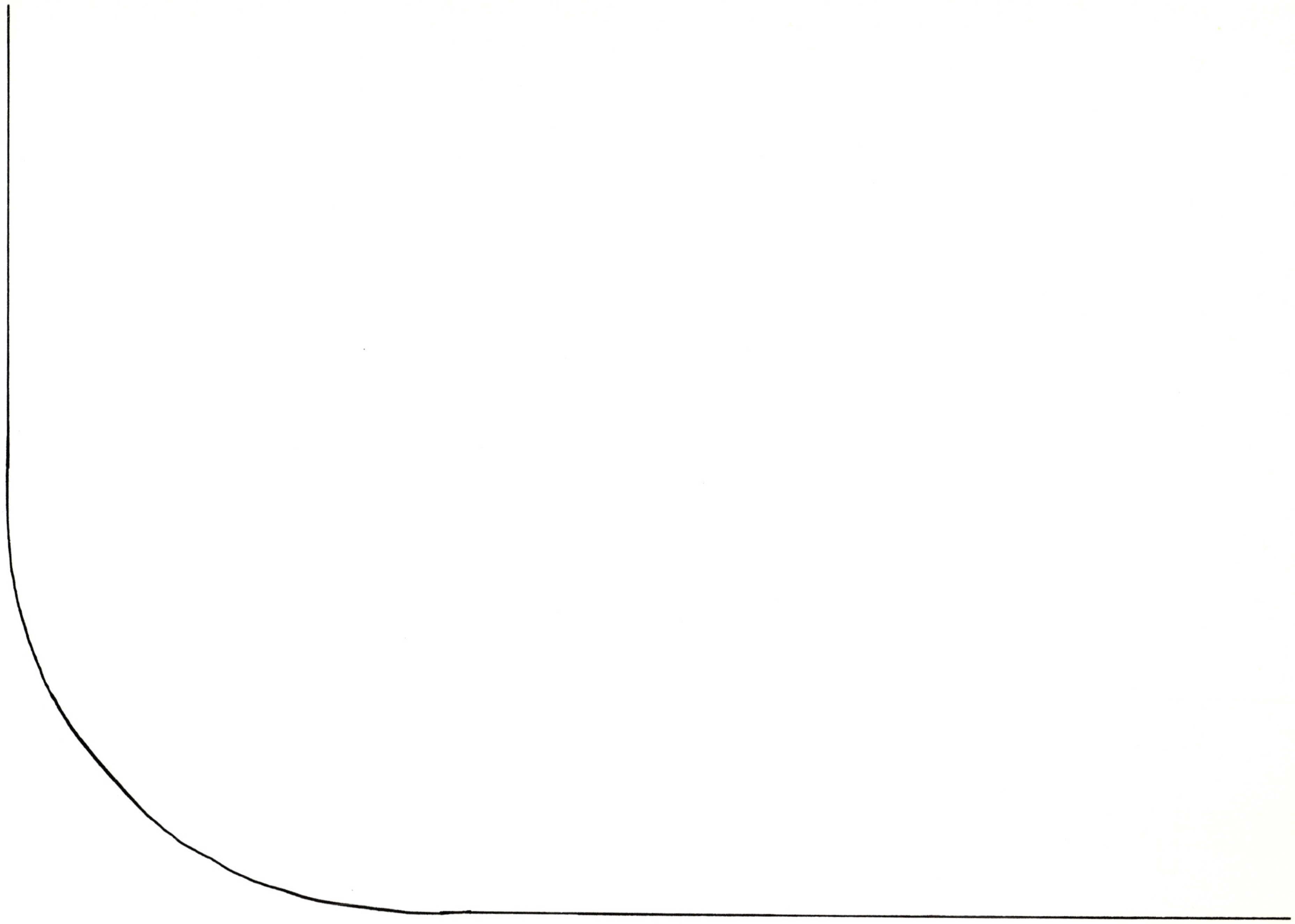

Figure 5(f). Mirror 24" x 36", Rounded at All Corners

Illustration 2-21

Illustration 2-22

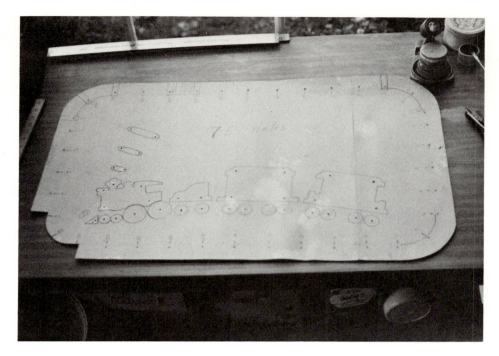

Illustration 2-23

Illustration 2-24

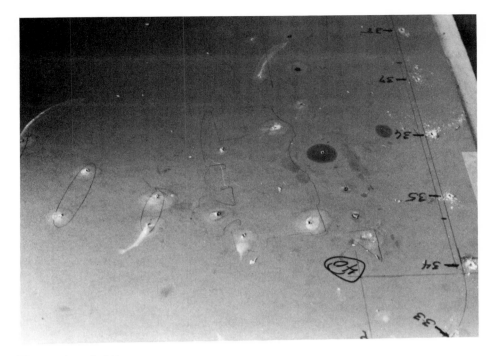

Illustration 2-25

Illustration 2-26

Illustration 2-27

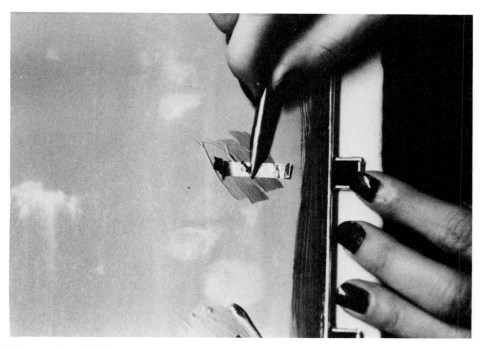

Illustration 2-28

Illustration 2-29

Illustration 2-30

Illustration 2-31

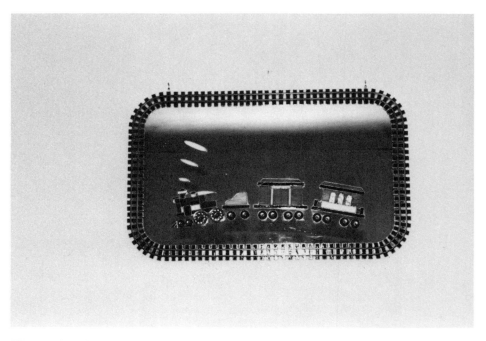

Illustration 2-32

6. Turn your mirror over and apply the Glass Pro Silver Protector around each hole and the edge of the mirror which will prevent the flux from eating away the mercury and causing black spots on the front of the mirror.
7. Take all your individual pieces of glass, place them in their corresponding holes, and tape them securely to the mirror.
8. Turn the mirror over, and pull through each pin with your pliers.
9. Overlay your 2-inch strips of foil around each pin and cut off $3/4$ inch on either side so that only $1/2$ inch of foil remains around each pin, and solder each pin to your strips of foil. (See Illustrations 2-27 through 2-29.)
10. Turn your mirror over again, and line up and tack solder from the top each railroad tie to the foil surrounding the mirror. (See Illustration 2-30.)
11. Your railroad track—2 strips of H came—must now be carefully stretched and laid down over your black ties. Use a metal straightedge as a guide when you tack solder the H came to the ties. When you shape the came around the corners, use the cutout of the template as a pattern. (See Illustration 2-31.)
12. You will need to attach secure brass stripping to support the considerable weight of the mirror. Take two pieces of brass stripping, bent in half, and attach to both horizontal ends of the mirror at the edge of the railroad tie pins. Then solder a brass rod with a loop in the middle upon which the mirror will hang.

This brass rod will distribute the weight of the mirror over a broader surface. You do not want your train to derail and crash down into a thousand pieces; so take special care to securely fix this brass rod to your mirror. (See Illustration 2-32.)

3

Three-Dimensional Projects

The key to building three-dimensional objects is in the *reinforcement of your structure*. Glass and solder are *heavy*. The weight of these materials in conjunction with the angles at which you attach your glass pieces or other substances combine to cause myriad structural problems if their pressure and weight is not distributed evenly. Just as you reinforced your lampshades to prevent them from crashing down on your dinner guest's roast beef, you must prevent fracturing and collapse of these projects by relieving unnatural stress at critical junctures.

Our three projects — the Parrot, Terrarium, and Clock — will introduce you to various reinforcement techniques and materials and provide you with a good base for your own variation on our theme. Since most of us come equipped with only two hands, our instructions will assume that you are executing them solo and will need other materials to hold your glass at the proper angles. (Of course, if you can acquire another cooperative set of hands, the actual construction steps will be much simplified.)

The Caged Parrot

Tools and Materials. We will assume that you have the basic glass cutting and soldering tools, and that you know where to acquire glass, solder, and copper foil (since all three of our 3-D projects are foiled, not camed). We have indicated quantities and suggested type and color of glass and materials on the pattern sheets. Only the unique materials and tools needed for each specific project will be discussed in this section:

Brass Ring. 8-inch by 10-inch diameter, *solid* brass. We suggest that you buy a solid brass rather than a brass-plated ring because the brass-finished steel will not readily accept the solder. You will have to scrape off the brass to get down to the undermetal and then tin it *before* you attempt to solder anything to it. You can do this, but it is much easier if you use a solid-brass ring, which requires no scraping and accepts the solder easily. You can purchase this and all the rest of the brass at a good-quality crafts or hobby store.

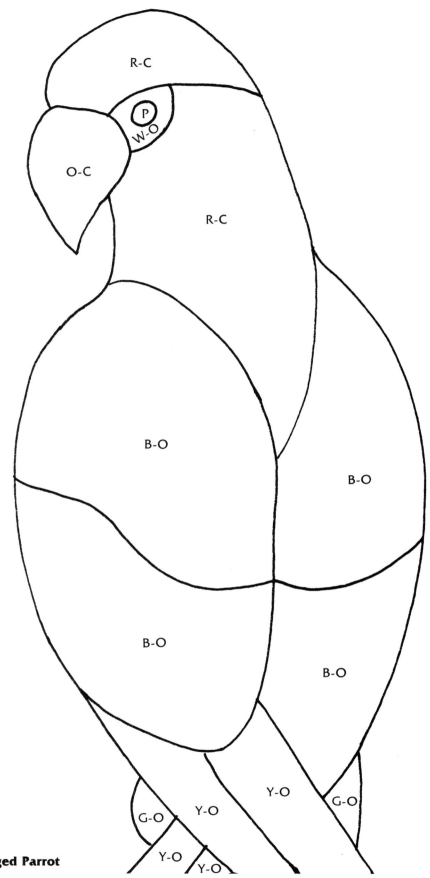

Figure 6. The Caged Parrot

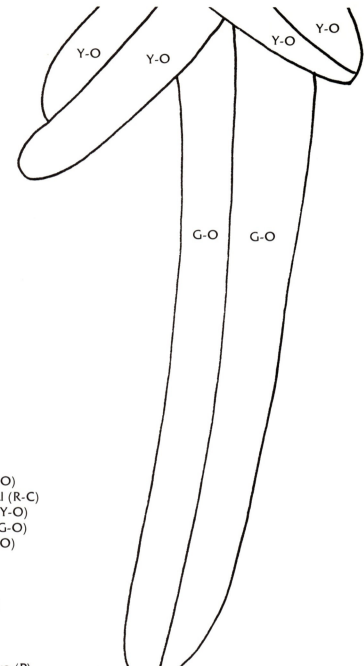

MATERIALS

Glass
1/2 sq. ft. Blue Opal (B-O)
1/2 sq. ft. Red Cathedral (R-C)
1/2 sq. ft. Yellow Opal (Y-O)
1/2 sq. ft. Green Opal (G-O)
scrap — White Opal (W-O)

Other
1 roll U hobby came
1 roll, 7/32" copper foil
1 brass rod
1 9" brass ring
1 brass sheet
　(thin black paint for eye (P)

Figure 6(a).　The Caged Parrot (2-pp spread)

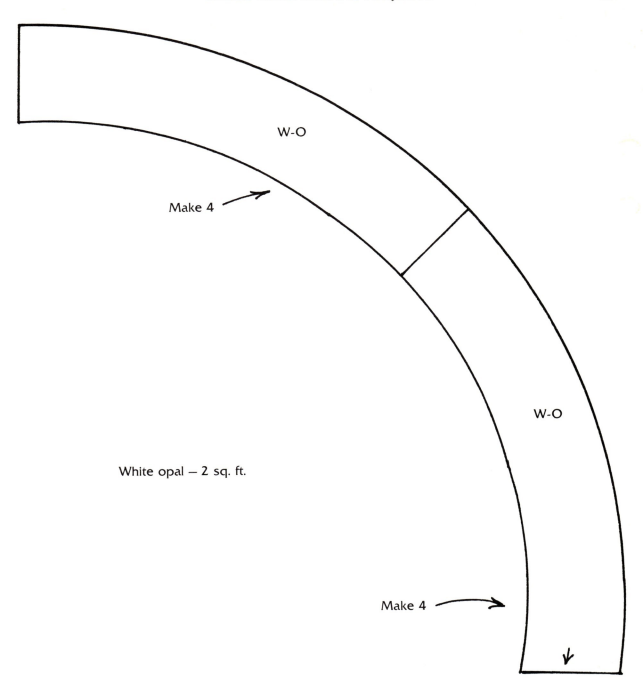

Figure 6(b).   Parrot Cage Bars

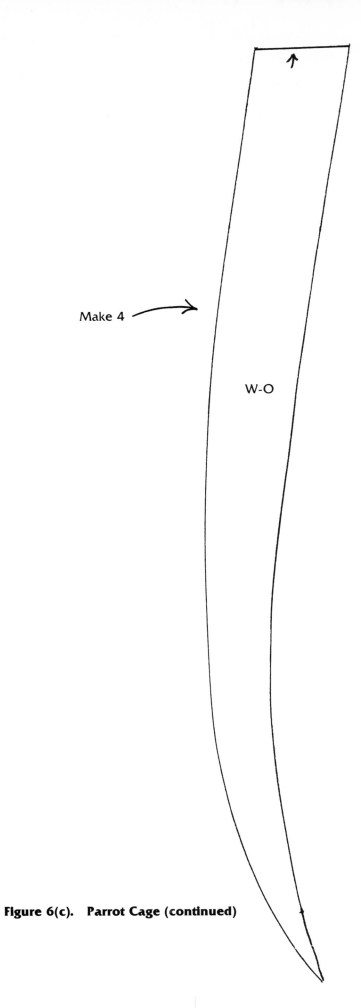

Make 4

W-O

Figure 6(c). Parrot Cage (continued)

Brass Tubing. One 3-foot strip, $1/4$ inch diameter. This tubing will act as a turning sleeve for the parrot cage to rotate.

Brass Brazing Rod. One 3-foot strip, $1/32$ inch or $1/16$ inch diameter. This will be your stabilizing and hanging material.

Flat Sheet Brass. One strip, $3^3/4$ inches or so wide, 9–10 inches long, .015 inch thick. You will overlay strips of this to strengthen and reinforce the white cage's adherence to the brass rod and tubing.

Heavy Scissors or Tin Snips. The flat brass sheets must be cut into thin strips with either of these tools.

Drill and ⅛-inch Bit. Refer to our discussion of drilling techniques in our Blind Soldering chapter, pp. 52–53.

TOOLS AND MATERIALS

Tool/Material	Brand/Description	Available At . . .
A. THE CAGED PARROT		
Brass ring	8″ × 10″ diameter	Quality craft supplier
Brass tubing	1/8″ diameter, 3′ long	Quality craft supplier
Brass braising rod	1/16″ or 1/32″ diameter	Quality craft supplier
Brass sheet	1 strip — .015″ thick, 10″ long, 33/4″ wide	Quality craft supplier
Good scissors or tin snips	Medium-sized	Hardware store
Electric drill	Hand-held or drill press (See Blind Soldering, page 49)	Retail or hardware store
1/8″ bit	Carbide	Hardware store
Wire cutter or dyke	Small	Hardware store

METHODS

1. Cut out your parrot, foil the pieces, flux and solder it, wrap it with came, patina it if you choose, clean it thoroughly, and place it aside for awhile.

    2. Cut out your four cage bars, foil them, and solder them individually. *Do not solder them together.* Place them safely aside. (See Illustration 3-1.)

    3. Put the brass ring and brazing rod on the table.

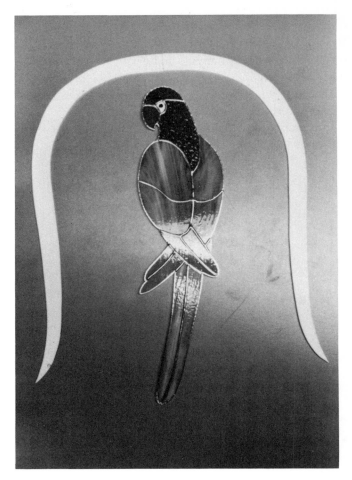

Illustration 3-1

4. Cut about an 8-inch piece of brazing rod and solder it to the top of the brass ring. This will be the main support by which you will hang the parrot; *so make sure that you solder it securely.* Put the ring/rod aside.

5. Lay out two cage bars flat on the table with the tops nearly touching.

6. Cut a piece of brass tubing the exact width (1 inch) of the top part of the strips and place it between the two strips.

7. Flux and solder securely the white cage bars to the brass tubing. (See Figure 6 (d).)

8. Solder the two remaining cage strips to the brass tubing opposite the other soldered pair.

9. Cut a 6-inch strip of brass plating with a rounded edge in the middle (pattern on pg. 81) the same thickness as your cage bars (you will have to measure your glass thickness — usually $^1/_{16}$ inch–$^1/_8$ inch.)

10. Drill a hole the same diameter as your brass tubing ($^1/_8$ inch or $^1/_4$ inch) in the center of the rounded portion of your brass strip.

11. Drop the brass plating strip over the brazing rod/brass tubing, on top, overlaying the edges of an adjoining pair of cage strips. (See Illustration 3-2.)

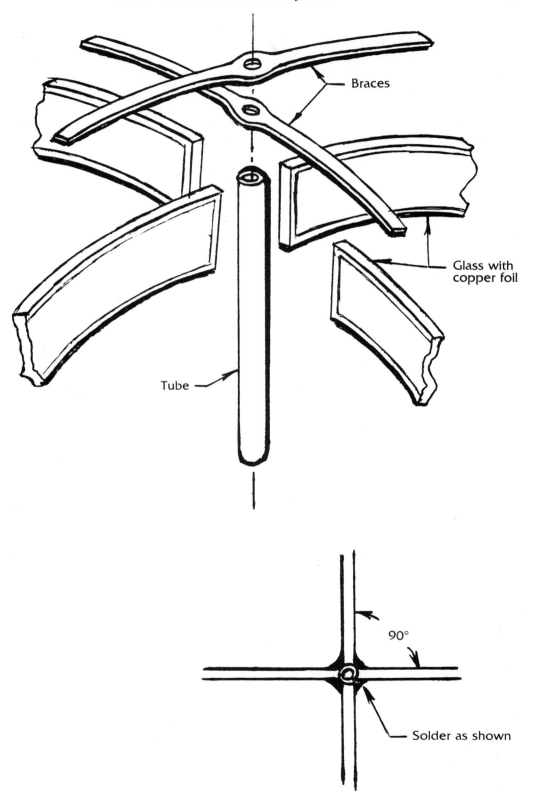

Braces

Glass with copper foil

Tube

90°

Solder as shown

Figure 6(d). Assembling Parrot Cage

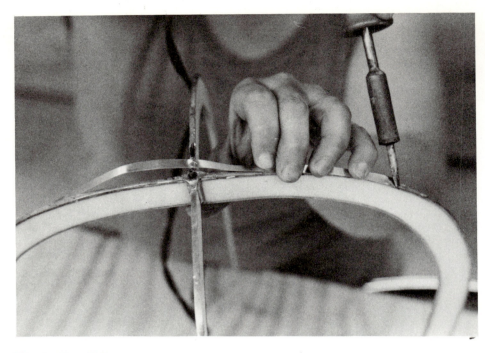

Illustration 3-2

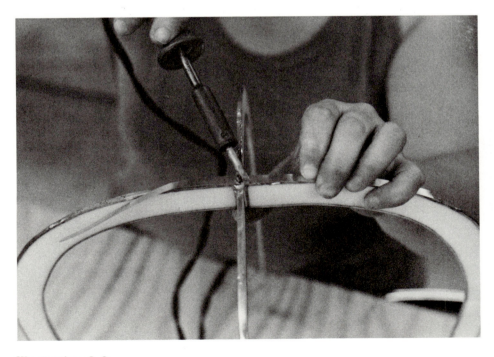

Illustration 3-3

12. Flux and solder the brass plating along the edges of the cage strips. This is the second critical reinforcing stage, so exercise care and exactness. (See Illustration 3-3.)

13. Repeat steps 11 and 12 to the other pair of cage strips. Make sure that all the brass stripping is soldered over and attached to the brass tubing and/or a piece of glass.

14. Solder the parrot to the brass ring at its feet. (See Illustration 3-4.)

15. Measure and cut off a piece of brazing rod from the parrot's head to the top of the ring. Solder at both points in order to stabilize the parrot on the ring. (See Illustration 3-5.)

16. Drop your brass tubing/cage bars section over the brass rod, down to the top of the ring. (See Illustration 3-6.)

17. With a pair of pliers, bend the top of the excess brazing rod to form a hook from which you can hang the parrot and his cage. (See Illustration 3-7.)

You should now have a stable parrot in a rotating cage that has been reinforced with various brass elements at its point of greatest stress — the junction of the cage and parrot at the main hanging point. (See Illustration 3-8.)

If you have foiled correctly and soldered thoroughly, this parrot and cage should hang anywhere for many years with little chance of ever coming apart.

The Canopy Terrarium

The key factor in this project is the need for support materials both in construction and in the finished project since it will be quite heavy when completed and filled with soil and a plant. As with lampshade construction, we have found various-sized buckets to be an invaluable tool for maintaining proper glass angles and holding tack-soldered pieces together. The other "unique" tools don't really warrant detailed discussion here since we have mentioned their main function elsewhere. Our listing in the chart (page 95) and in the procedure should be sufficient. (See Figures 7 (a) to (c).)

It is best to approach our terrarium in three stages, with the bowl (bottom) as our first:

BOWL

1. Naturally, cut out all the pieces of the entire terrarium first. It is *extremely important* that all the pieces be as nearly exactly the same as possible. You want smooth, straight edges especially, so be certain to use a straightedge. (See lampshade panel cutting, pp. 7–8.)

2. Foil all your pieces, making sure that your glass is clean when foiling and that the foil adheres tightly and smoothly to the glass.

3. Draw the pattern of your hexagon base on a large piece of wood.

4. Place a pushpin behind the *center* of each side (panel) *on the outside of the line.*

5. Take two panels of the planter base, place them together inside the pins against the pins until their two inner seams combine to make one. Use the same technique as outlined in our panel lampshade section, pp. 10–13.

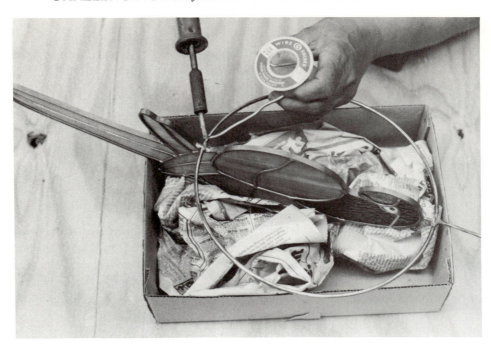

Illustration 3-4

Illustration 3-5

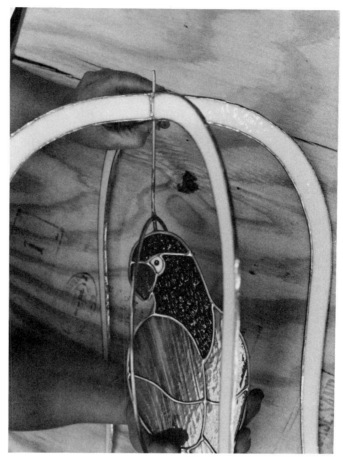

Illustration 3-6

6. One-quarter inch from the top and bottom and in the center of the seam, *on the inside seam,* tack solder the two pieces together.

7. Continue around the base of the terrarium, tack soldering all the base panels, resting the soldered panels against the pushpins. (See Illustration 3-9.)

8. Place a piece of glass under your completed ring (smaller circumference on the bottom), and trace the opening, *on both the outside and inside of the ring,* creating a double line. (See Illustrations 3-10 and 3-11.)

9. Cut your bottom by scoring *directly in the middle* of the dual line. This will ensure an almost perfect fit.

10. Completely solder the bottom to the ring and place the finished bowl aside. (See Illustration 3-12.)

CANOPY

1. Now pick up two triangular canopy sides, angle and join them together, and tack-solder them ($^1/_4$ inch from top and bottom, and center) *on the outside.*

Illustration 3-7

2. Place pushpins at the outside center that will act as a frame to each panel maintaining the proper angle. (See lampshade panel construction, pp. 10–13, for the technique for steps 1–6. See Illustration 3-13.)

3. Tack-solder the entire canopy together.

4. Gently place the canopy, *point down*, in a bucket. This will prevent the pieces from shifting and separating and also hold the canopy in a true circle.

5. Tack-solder with globs of solder 1 inch apart the entire inside of the canopy.

6. Take the canopy out of the bucket and repeat step 5 on the outside and place it upside down again in the bucket.

7. Take your washer, and steelwool the finish off, clean it, and then apply a coat of solder all over it (tinning).

8. Place your washer down on the inside at the opening of your canopy. Place your electrical nipple through the washer/opening and tighten it snugly to the washer, with your electrical nuts at both ends. *Do not overtighten* because you may break glass or spread your soldered seams apart. (See Illustration 3-14.)

9. Solder securely every abutting joint/seam to your washer and place your canopy aside with your bowl. (See Illustration 3-15.)

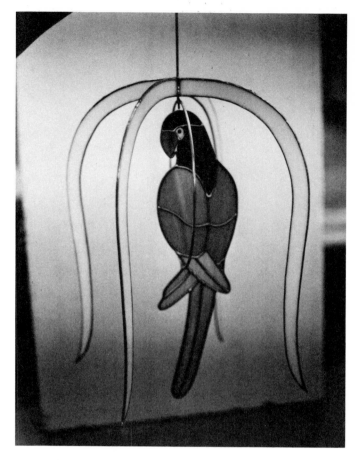

Illustration 3-8

SIDES

1. Pick up one long panel, and a "cutout," and clamp them (or have someone hold them) so that the edges touch at the correct angle. (See Illustration 3-16.)

2. Tack-solder them together in the usual manner (as with panel lampshades and the canopy) *on the inside.* (See Illustration 3-17.)

3. Continue all around, taking a long piece and a cutout and tack-solder all these pieces together.

4. Turn the side section upside down and insert the 4 remaining cutouts and tack solder them onto the structure.

You should now have three separate sections tack-soldered together and ready for assembly:

1. Put your bowl on your worktable in front of you.

2. Place the sides (middle) section with the smaller cutout directly on top of

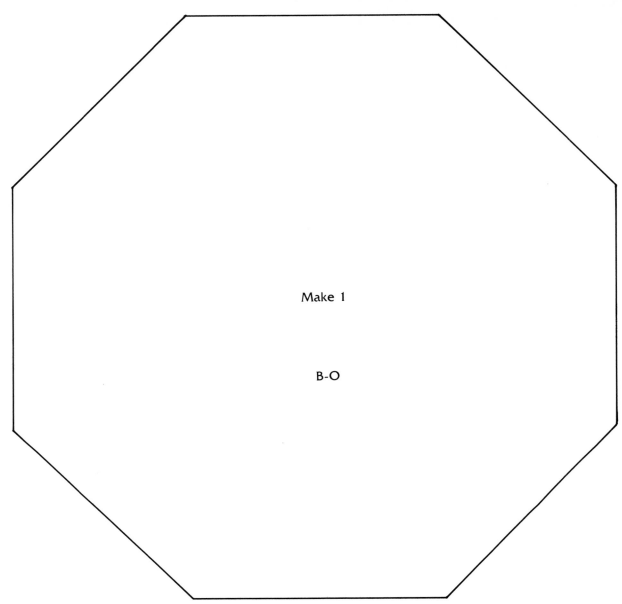

Make 1

B-O

Materials

4 sq. ft. Blue Opal (B-O)
2 sq. ft. Blue Seedy (B-S)
1 roll, 1/4" foil
1 1/2 lbs., 60/40 solder
1 medium brass rod
1 large washer

Figure 7(a). The Canopy Terrarium — The Hexagon Base

Make 4 solid panels

Make 4 panels with cut-outs

Material
2 sq. ft. Blue Seedy (B-S)

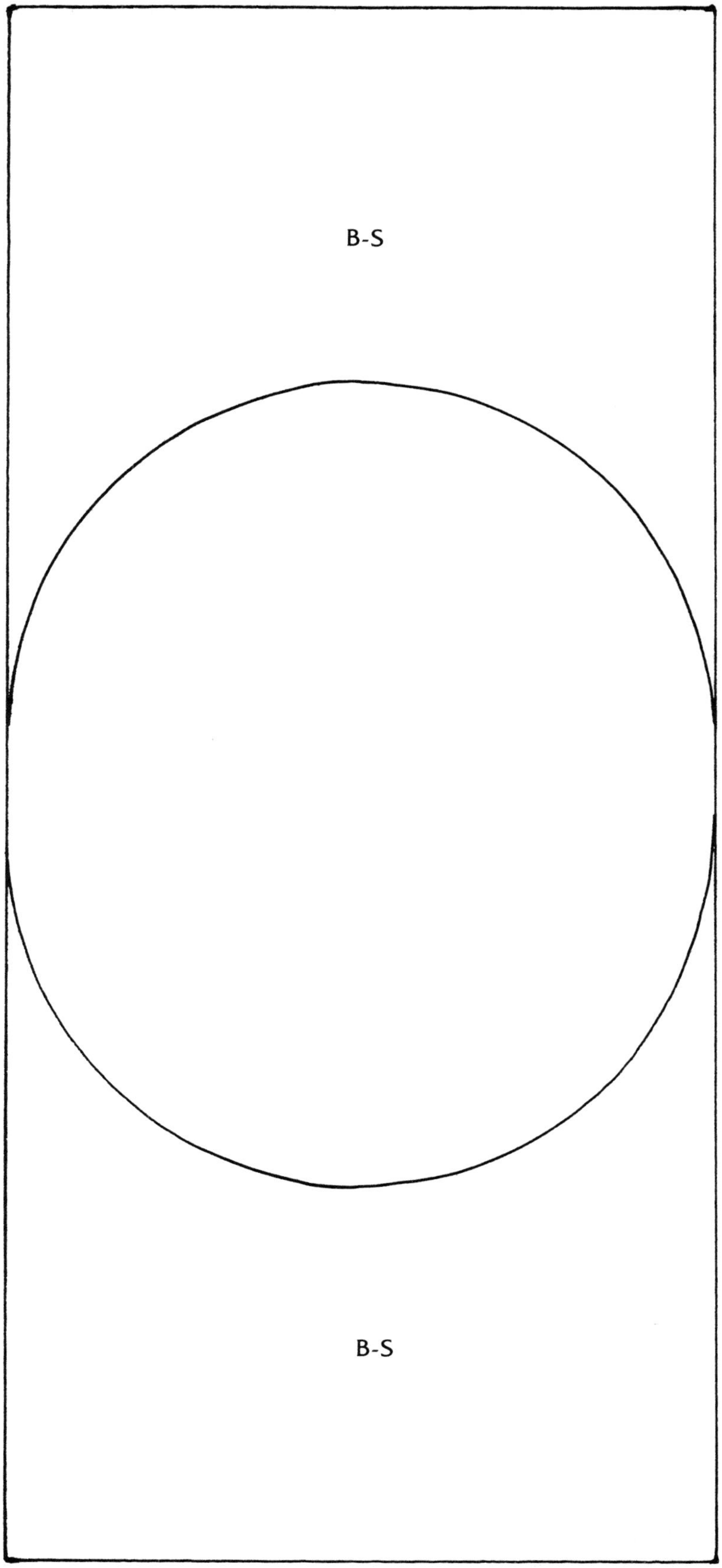

B-S

B-S

Figure 7(b). The Base Panels

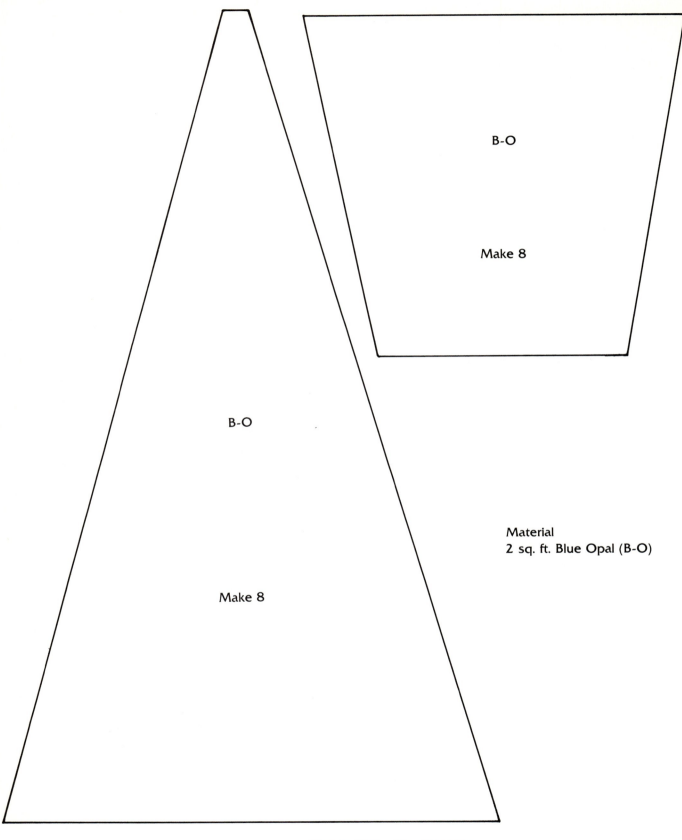

B-O

Make 8

B-O

Make 8

Material
2 sq. ft. Blue Opal (B-O)

Figure 7(c). The Canopy

TOOLS AND MATERIALS

Tool/Material	Brand/Description	Available At . . .
B. THE CANOPY TERRARIUM		
Brass braising rod	See above	See above
Washer	1 1/2″ diameter, with 3/8″ or 7/16″ hole in center	Hardware store
One electrical coupling nipple	2″ length, 3/8″ thread	Electrical supply store
Two electrical coupling nuts	Standard size for nipple	Electrical supply store
Plastic buckets	Varying sizes	Bakeries, restaurants, building suppliers
Clamps	Stanley friction clamp	Hardware store
Tongue depressor or popsickle stick	Notched with a razorblade at the tip	Medical supply or grocery store
Push pins	One box, 5/8″ leg, steel head	Stationery or office supply store
Steelwool	000-extra-fine	Hardware supply store

Illustration 3-9

Illustration 3-10

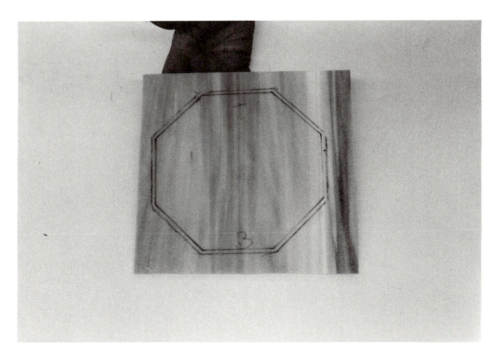

Illustration 3-11

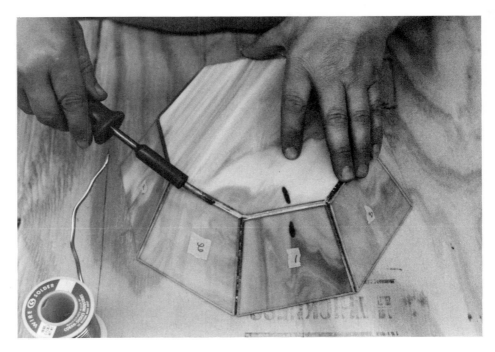

Illustration 3-12

Illustration 3-13

Illustration 3-14

Illustration 3-15

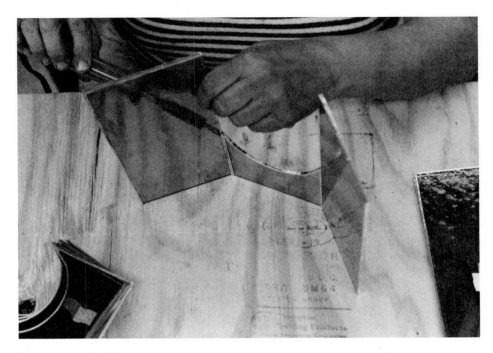

Illustration 3-16

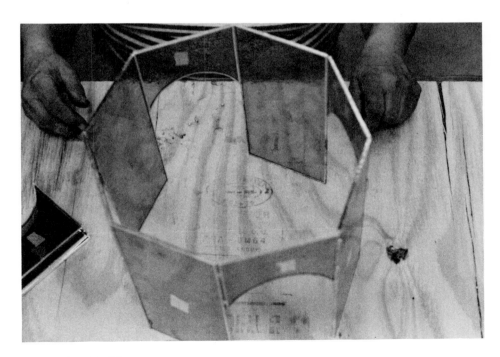

Illustration 3-17

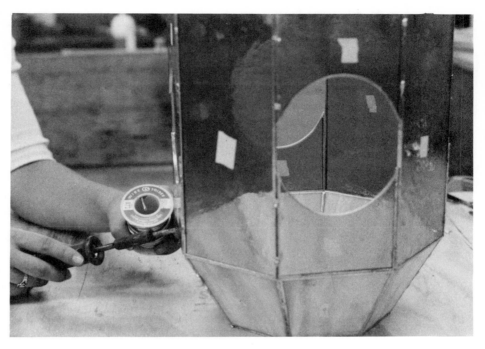

Illustration 3-18

your bowl, adjusting the joints/seams of both until they align themselves as closely as possible. (See Illustration 3-18.)

3. Tack-solder (globs 1 inch apart) your bowl and sides together.

4. Put your canopy point-down into the bucket again.

5. Place your bowl/sides section into your canopy, lining up the foiled seams of the canopy to your side component. (See Illustration 3-19.)

6. To ensure that your bowl/side section is standing straight, measure the distance from a side section to the outside of the canopy. Do the same with the side opposite to this first panel. Adjust the bowl/side section until every measurement is equal (you should only have to do this two or three times on two opposite sets of panels). (See Illustration 3-20.)

7. Now that the bowl/side section is standing straight, tack-solder on *the outside only* all the canopy and bowl/side joining seams.

REINFORCEMENT

8. Here is where your brass brazing rod comes in. Cut a strip about 6 inches long and bend with your pliers in the center (to produce 2 three-inch lengths) to correspond to the inside pitch of the canopy and the adjoining inside side section seam.

9. You are going to overlay this braising rod on to the *center of the inside side/canopy seam* by holding it down tightly with your notched tongue depressor and

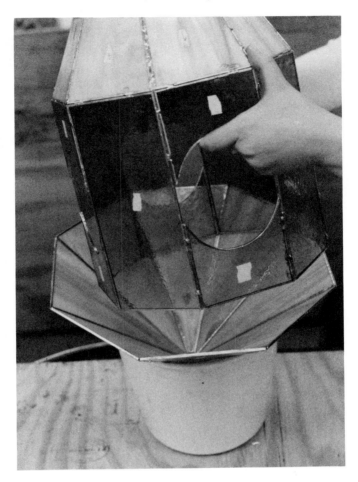

Illustration 3-19

fluxing and tack-soldering it in place, just as you did with the lampshades, on pages 11 and 13.

10. Repeat steps 8 and 9 with the remaining seven seams.

11. Finish soldering over all eight brass rods, so that the braising rods are not noticeable and you have one smooth-flowing seam.

12. Now completely solder the entire terrarium by manipulating the terrarium inside the bucket and on your worktable (in a similar fashion to the technique outlined in the Lampshade chapter, page 19. (See Illustration 3-21.)

13. If you choose, you can wrap U lead came around the window opening and canopy edge by stripping the foil with a razorblade and soldering the lead to an intersecting soldered seam. (See the discussion of this technique in our Lampshade section, pp. 24 and 26.) Use dabs of "527 Bond" glue inside your channels to cement the lead to the canopy. Keep glue away from the areas that are to be soldered.

Your Canopy Terrarium should now be completely soldered and strongly reinforced. Those brass brazing rods will support the entire weight when the terrarium is planted because it equally distributes the weight to eight different points.

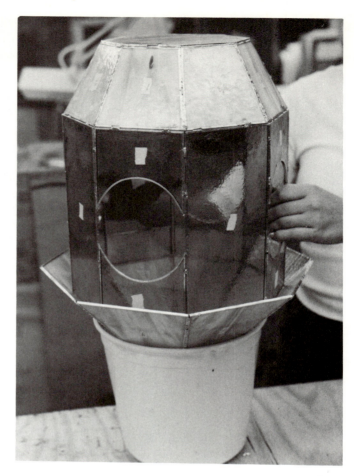

Illustration 3-20

By attaching a metal ring on top, you can hang the terrarium as is or bring it down to an electrical supply store where an accommodating clerk will sell you the necessary equipment: e.g., socket, wire, etc., to create an interesting and brightly lit terrarium. (See Illustration 3-22.)

The Floral Clock

This clock will extend your stained glass capabilities in creating something in the same functional or practical vein as the lampshade and terrarium. The unique dimension of this project is its relatively inexpensive but extremely reliable, battery-operated, quartz clockworks. It should also spur your imagination to try to provide other motor- or battery-driven applications to stained glass projects. *It can be done!* (See Figures 8 (a) through (i).)

Illustration 3-21

To begin:

1. First, you will have to drill a 3/8-inch hole in the middle of your clock face so that you can insert your clockworks (hands). If you want to do it yourself, refer to our directions for drilling with carbide or diamond bits in the Blind Soldering chapter (pages 52–54). Or, you can bring the glass to a regular glass shop and, for a small price, they will drill the hole for you.

IMPORTANT NOTE: Do not cut your glass to the exact size of the face pattern of our clock until *after* you've drilled the hole. Take a piece of glass 12 inches by 12 inches, draw a diagonal line through it to find the center, and drill your hole where the lines intersect. Then, using the hole as the center point, place our pattern over the glass, outline it, and cut out the exact size.

2. Cut and foil your individual pieces for the clock base and border, adjusting the pattern, if necessary, to correlate to your clock face. (See Illustration 3-23.)

3. Cut, wrap, and solder your pair of flowers and put aside. These flowers will be overlaid and soldered right to the clock afterward. (See Illustration 3-24.)

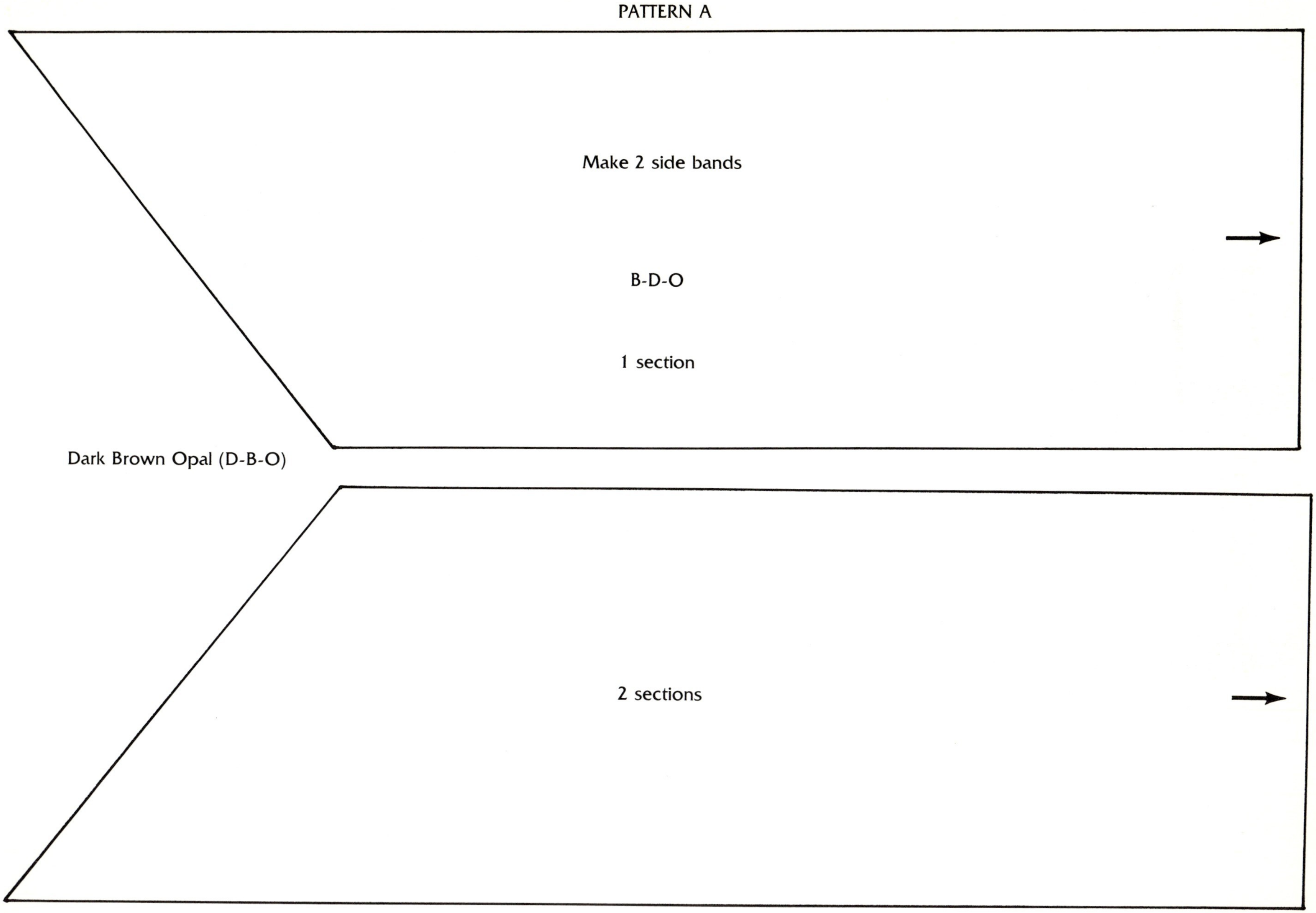

PATTERN A

Make 2 side bands

B-D-O

1 section

2 sections

Dark Brown Opal (D-B-O)

Figure 8(a). The Floral Clock – Pattern A

Illustration 3-22

Illustration 3-23

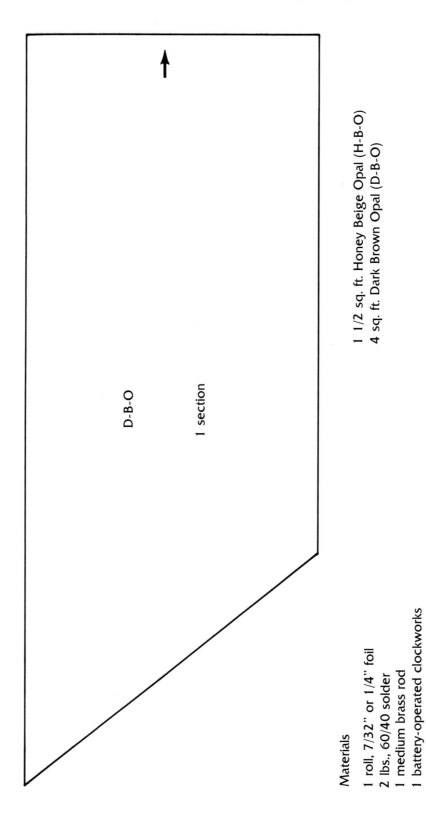

PATTERN B

D-B-O

1 section

1 1/2 sq. ft. Honey Beige Opal (H-B-O)
4 sq. ft. Dark Brown Opal (D-B-O)

Materials

1 roll, 7/32" or 1/4" foil
2 lbs., 60/40 solder
1 medium brass rod
1 battery-operated clockworks

Figure 8(b). Pattern B

PATTERN C

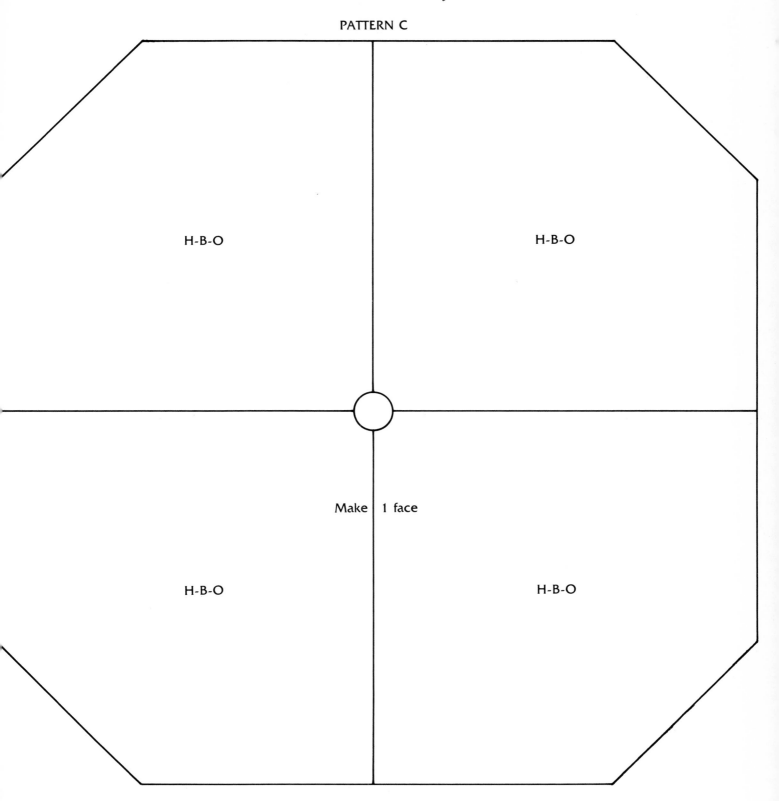

Figure 8(c). Pattern C — The Face

PATTERN D

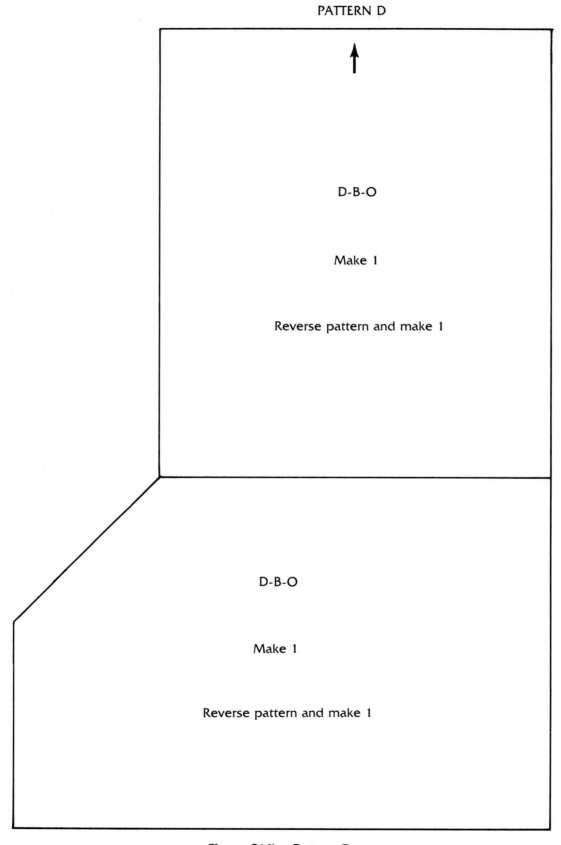

Figure 8(d).   Pattern D

PATTERN E

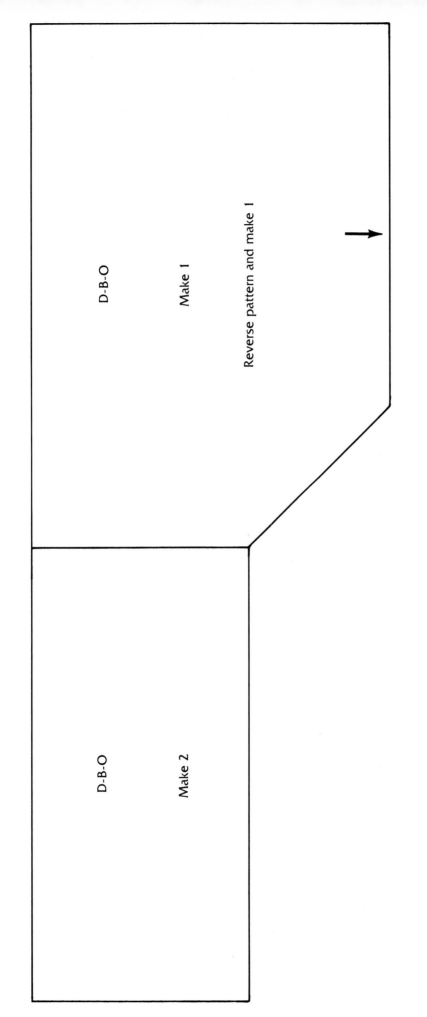

D-B-O

Make 1

Reverse pattern and make 1

D-B-O

Make 2

Figure 8(e). Pattern E

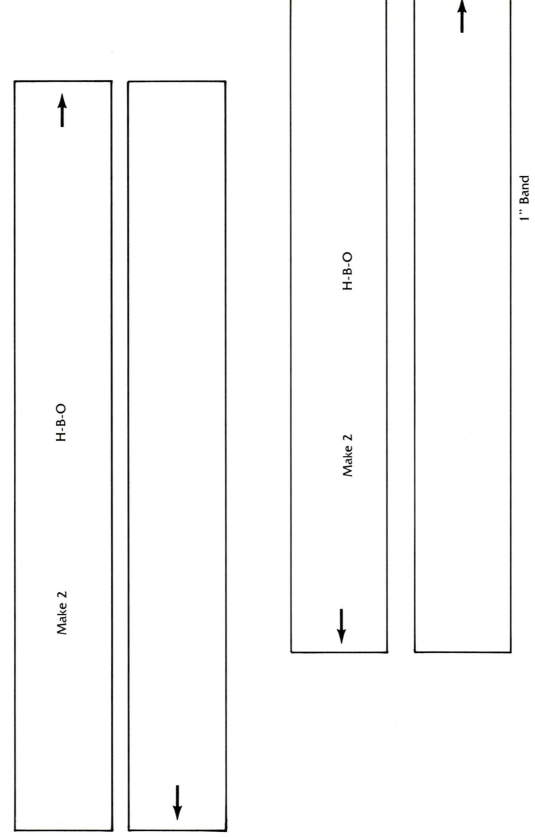

Figure 8(f).   Pattern F

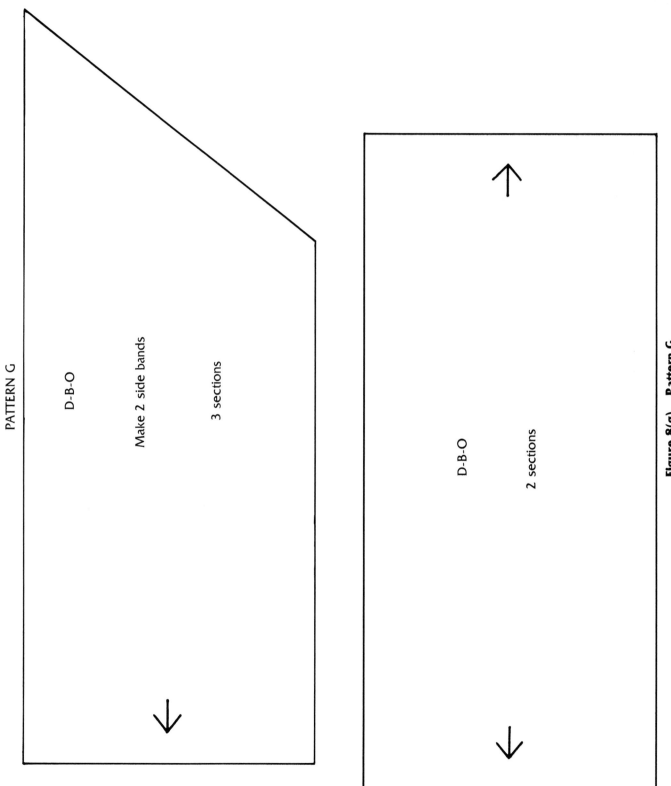

PATTERN G

D-B-O

Make 2 side bands

3 sections

D-B-O

2 sections

Figure 8(g). Pattern G

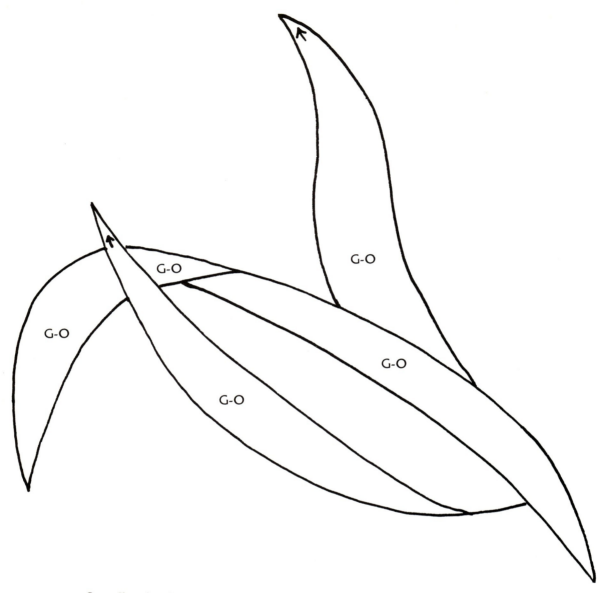

Supplies for flowers

Make 2 sets of flowers

1 small sheet Green Opal (G-O)
1 small sheet Orange Opal (O-O)
1 small sheet Yellow Opal (Y-O)
1 small sheet Peach Opal (P-O)

Figure 8(h).   Pattern for Flower — 1

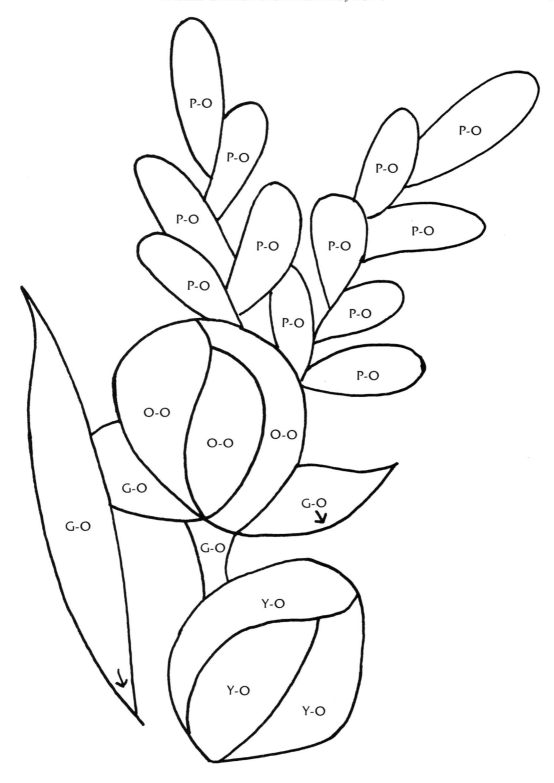

Figure 8(i). Pattern for Flower — 2

TOOLS AND MATERIALS

Tool/Material	Brand/Description	Available At . . .
C. THE FLORAL CLOCK		
Battery-operated quartz clockworks	German-made	Clock repair shop or clock supplier
Drilling materials (optional)	See Blind Soldering, page 49	
Braising rod	See above	
Mirror protector	**Glass Pro** silver protector	Stained glass supplier or glass company

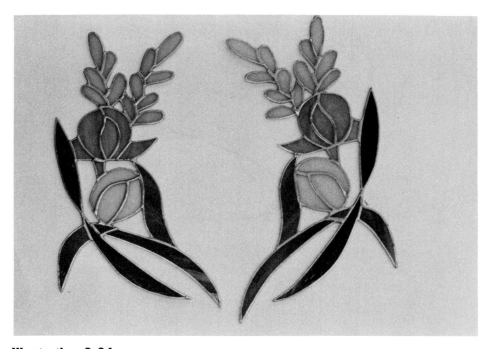

Illustration 3-24

4. Solder (on both sides) and assemble the face and adjoining flat border around the face.
5. Turn your assembled face and flat border upside down on your table.
6. Take two mitred border pieces, lay them flat and butting two joining edges, and raise them until their edges meet at the corners of the assembled clockpiece. (See Illustration 3-25.)

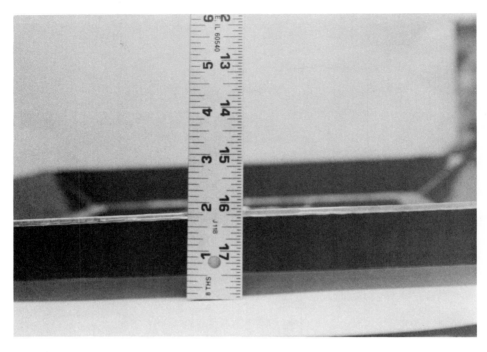

Illustration 3-25

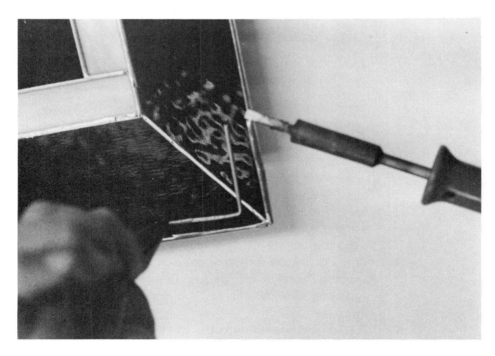

Illustration 3-26

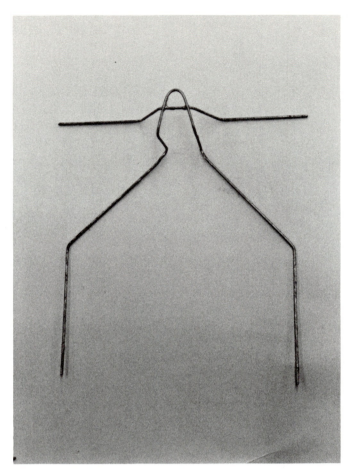

Illustration 3-27

7. Tack-solder *on the outside* with globs of solder one inch apart.
8. Shape with your pliers a 4-inch (or the length of your inside corner seam) piece of brass brazing rod or a small, thin wire to fit an inside corner seam.
9. Tack-solder the braising rod to the inside corner. (See Illustration 3-26.)
10. Repeat steps 8 and 9 for the three remaining corners.
11. Finish soldering your entire project. Lead-came or solder the clock edges and patina if you wish.
12. Clean thoroughly.
13. Form a bent loop with your pliers in a braising rod (similar to one pictured) by which the clock will hang on the wall. (See Illustration 3-27.) Solder the rod at least 4 inches into two solder seams/joints for sufficient strength. (See Illustration 3-28.)
14. Overlay the flowers onto the clock face by tack soldering *with small, neat joints* at every intersecting foil seam where the Clock face and flowers meet. (See Illustration 3-29.)

Illustration 3-28

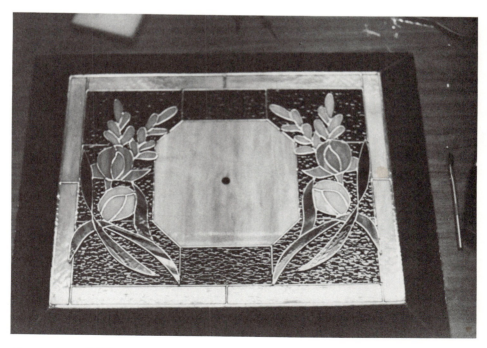

Illustration 3-29

Illustration 3-30

15. Install your clockworks now according to the manufacturer's instructions. *Do not overtighten or your clock face might fracture.* (See Illustration 3-30.)
NOTE: You must protect your clockworks and especially the hands from damage. This is the main reason we have saved this step for last, even though there is a slight chance that your face may fracture. If you tried soldering, finishing, and cleaning your project *after* you insert your clockworks, there is a good chance of your damaging some delicate part.

Summing Up

The world of three-dimensional stained glass projects is limited only by your imagination. If properly braced, three-dimensional structures can be as practical or as aesthetically pleasing as any made with other materials.

Flat pieces of glass can be used in the same manner as wood or metal; and they can be shaped (see the chapter on Glass Bending) as well for any purpose, provided that you have the tools and equipment. We hope we have stretched the possibilities of your glass skills by exposing you to this relatively unexplored stained glass territory.

4

Bent Glass

After attempting all that you can do with flat glass, the logical progression would be toward bent and blown glass. While we have not experimented enough with blown glass (stay tuned, however) to include a chapter in this book, we do believe that we can introduce you to the very exciting world of bent and molded glass in itself and its unique applications to and combinations with flat glass projects.

We could probably write an entire book on this subject alone, but because of time and space limitations, we are only going to cover what we think you will need to know to get involved with bent-panel lampshades, terrariums, and three-dimensional projects. These procedures and instructions, coupled with their application to a lampshade or three-dimensional project should whet your appetite and provide incentive to pursue your own course of personal experimentation and further education.

Tools and Materials

The Kiln. Undoubtedly, this is the most expensive piece of equipment needed for bending glass. There are various companies who manufacture various types. Rather than listing them all, or discussing the pros and cons of each, we will describe the kiln we use and tell you why we use it. After reading what we have to say, and then researching kiln information on your part, you can choose your own kiln.

We use a top-loading kiln (which usually has two very important peepholes) rather than one with an ovenlike, front-loading door. (See Illustration 4-1). The process of bending the glass, and then cooling it down, should be gradual. With a front-loading kiln, the minute you open the door a burst of relatively cool air will rush in and, in effect, traumatize the hot glass to such a point that the bending/melting, or annealing processes would be severely and adversely affected. Whereas with the top-loading kiln, the heat from the bottom of the kiln would rise, preventing a shock of cold air from forcing itself in. A top-loader would also ensure a gradual cooling down of the glass to room temperature, thus making both processes less complicated and improving the chances of success.

Which *size* kiln is best? We use a kiln with an 18″ × 18″ oven diameter. This larger size will not limit you for most projects and allow you to create larger projects and

Illustration 4-1

panels for lampshades. We are constantly bombarded with requests from owners and antique dealers to create new panels to replace broken ones. This demand in itself has dictated our choice to a great extent, but has also paid for the kiln many times over.

Most of the kilns used for firing ceramics use pyrometric cones for monitoring and measuring heat levels. It is a pyramid-shaped material that acts like a timer to indicate when the kiln is at the desired temperature; it melts and automatically shuts off the kiln. However, because the temperature parameters for bending the glass have to be more flexible and yet stable and precise than in firing ceramics, we would recommend that you buy and use a *pyrometer*. It is an instrument that is inserted through the upper peep hole into the kiln to give you an accurate temperature reading (both Fahrenheit and Centigrade) inside the kiln.

You should also purchase *shelves and shelf supports* upon which you'll place your molds and glass. The shelf height (1 to 6 inches) is set by adjusting the supporting ceramic legs. The sets of shelves and legs are necessary to properly place the molds in the relative center of the kiln. When bending the glass, you will need a consistently even temperature over the surface of the glass. Since heat rises, there will always be a

TOOLS AND MATERIALS

Tool/Material	Brand/Description	Available At . . .
Kiln	Top-loading, 18″ × 18″	Ceramic house Building supply store
Pyrometer	Tubular	Building supply store
Kiln shelves and supports	Adjustable, 1″–6″	Building supply store
Kiln wash		Building supply store
Plaster of Paris		Hardware store
Retarder		Hardware store
Slip		Ceramic house
Cardboard box	12″ deep	Grocery store
Sandpaper	007 grade	Hardware store

"cold" spot at the bottom of your kiln and, conversely, there will always be a "hot" spot at the top where the heat collects. Therefore, you should adjust your shelves so that your mold and glass is above at least two heating elements above the bottom cold spot, and 4 to 6 inches below the top of the door, so that your glass will be in the center where the temperature is most consistent. That is why we insert our pyrometer in the *top* peephole, in order to have an accurate reading of the temperature around the glass.

You will need also some *kiln wash* (purchased from the manufacturer or a ceramic house). This is a powder that can be shifted over a flat mold or mixed with water to a paint consistency and transferred to a contoured mold and allowed to dry. The kiln wash is a release agent for your glass which allows it to separate easily from your mold. It lasts through numerous firings and when it does begin to cause glass sticking, merely requires a washing off of the mold and a reapplication of the kiln wash.

That should be about it in regard to the kiln.

Molds. The making and shaping of the mold is the primary activity in the glass-bending process. The care and patience you exercise in the sculpturing of the mold will determine to a great extent the success of your finished product. You need to visualize in your mind what you want the glass to look like, and then sculpt a mold to which the glass will conform.

You must decide first whether you will want the glass to *sag into* a mold, or *drape over* the sides of the mold. If you are going to sag glass, you must remember two things.

it will slump or droop into a mold that will be the *obverse* or opposite of your intended finished project. In addition to conceptualizing and then creating the reverse or negative image, there is the possibility that trapped air in the recesses of the mold will create bubbles in your finished glass project. (If you do decide to sag or slump glass, you should drill small air holes to allow the air to escape as the glass conforms to the contour.)

It is because of these two reasons that we prefer to *drape* glass over the top and outside of a mold. We can create a true positive mold of what the finished project will be with little chance of bubbling.

You can visit a ceramic house, especially one that specializes in wholesaling molds, and purchase just about any shaped mold you would want. This would not be a bad idea for those first few experiments and projects, but we think that the most exciting part of bending glass is in the exercise of your creative imagination. Adopting other materials and constructing your own molds will introduce you to the infinite number of things you can accomplish with your kiln.

There are different techniques and materials employed when creating molds and we could describe most of them. But we believe the simplest method is to cast a master mold in *plaster of Paris* and then fashion a number of molds out of *slip* (a ceramic clay) from which your individual pieces can be fashioned and bent.

The first thing you should do is have a definite idea of what you want your finished project to look like. Sketch it out, mold it in children's clay, construct a paper model, whatever. Just make sure you know what you want your glass to look like before you attempt construction.

From your sketch or concrete concept of your finished project, you can sculpt a cast out of plaster of Paris. For those of you who have worked with plaster of Paris, you already know that it sets up (hardens) within five or ten minutes, not much time to form a cast by hand. To counteract its rapid setting, you can buy a small bag of *retarder* from a building supplier (the same place you bought your plaster of Paris) which will slow down its hardening time. It won't slow it down for hours, but to about ½ hour, which is ample time to realize your caste.

In our methods section (below), we outline simple techniques for casting master molds for some beginning projects and experiments. After doing it once or twice, you will be able to amplify and expand your own ideas following these basics.

By making many molds from the same cast or master, you can bend panels of glass in as many multiples as the capacity of your kiln will allow. This is a great time-saving technique when making lampshades or any project that requires repeated pieces.

Methods

After describing the preliminary steps of making a beginning cast and mold, we're going to cover the glass-bending process in three stages: (1) the firing of your kiln to reach the temperature at which your glass will begin to bend; (2) the annealing (hardening) stage; and (3) the gradual cooling down of the kiln and glass.

It must be emphasized here (before you really get into it) that these processes are not merely a matter of throwing switches on and off. During each process, which could last hours, *patient control of what occurs is the major component of each technique.* The complete process cannot be rushed; your anxious anticipation and desire to see your finished product must be suppressed and overcome by a more reasonable deference to time.

Besides, half the fun and satisfaction is conquering the many variables associated with the art of bending glass. Like Don Juan, the point of his seduction was not so much the bedding down of the unwilling lady, but the playing of the game itself.

One more NOTE: Every kiln, regardless of similar brands or models, has its own quirks and idiosyncracies that border on animateness. No two kilns, even if they are made and assembled by the same person, are exactly alike in the way they fire up and perform. We will relate how *our kiln* performs at different temperatures so you can have a relatively good starting point from which you can bracket temperatures and times. *You will have to keep notes and learn your kiln's idiosyncracies.* But, once you've become familiar with your kiln, you will get consistently good results and develop your interest and skills in glass bending to a point bordering on addiction.

Now, the making of a cast and mold.* You'll need a simple, half-circle cast:

1. Mix your plaster of Paris (without the retarder) in a bucket, pouring the water in first, then adding the plaster of Paris. Then pour it in a cardboard box the size of a case of beer, about half-filled.
2. Press a soccer ball or smooth round ball halfway down in the center of the plaster. Keep it there for about 10 minutes or until the plaster sets.
3. Remove the ball carefully.
4. Allow the plaster of Paris cast to dry *completely* (which usually takes about two days).
5. Then pour the slip into the mold and allow it to stand for 30 minutes. (The longer you allow the slip to set, the thicker your mold will be.)
6. Pour out the slip that has not set. This will leave you with a layer of hardened slip, usually ⅛ inch to ¼ inch thick, inside the hollow.
7. Without removing the slip mold, place the plaster cast in a "safe" place and allow the slip mold to harden for one or two days.
8. After the slip has hardened, *carefully* (because the mold is very brittle) remove the slip mold from the cast. The mold is now referred to as greenware.
9. With a very fine sandpaper, gently sand the greenware to make it as smooth as possible.
10. Wash it with a damp sponge and allow it to dry.
11. Place the greenware in your kiln and fire it at 1,200°(F) temperature for two hours. Allow the greenware to cool down before removing it from the kiln.
12. Apply kiln wash and allow it to dry.

Voilà! You now have a beautifully rounded greenware mold over which you will droop your glass for your initial firing experiments. This final step of firing your mold

---

*You can purchase a rounded mold at a ceramic house for these initial experiments if you don't want to build your own.

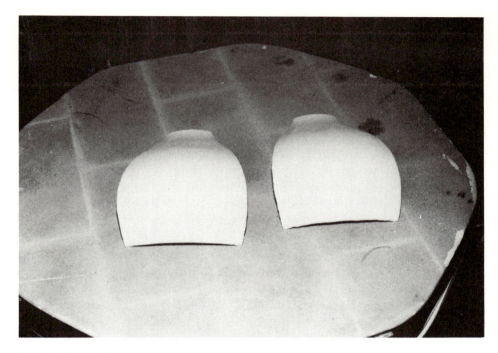

Illustration 4-2

has hardened it so that you can now handle it without fear of its cracking or breaking apart. (See Illustration 4-2). Now that your mold is ready, you can begin your firing and bending stage:

PLACEMENT

1. Place the mold on the bottom shelf in your kiln. The shelf should be above the first two heating elements.
2. Cut a *blank of glass.* Take a flat sheet and cut out a roughly estimated circle that will fit over the mold and not exceed or run over the bottom edge of the mold when it bends.
3. Balance the blank glass on top of the mold in the kiln.

VENTING

4. In order to *vent* the kiln to allow any pent up gasses from the hot mold and glass to escape, slowly raise the door about ½ inch and open your peepholes.
5. Insert your pyrometer in the peephole nearest the center of the kiln.
6. Turn on the bottom heating element only, and observe your kiln and pyrometer until the pyrometer reaches about 400°(F), a period of around 45 minutes.

7. Turn on your second element and allow the temperature to rise to about 800–900°(F), about one hour.
8. The gasses should be burnt off now so you should close your door and any open peephole tightly.

FIRING

9. When the temperature reaches 950°–1000° F), turn on the third heating element.

IMPORTANT: *Do not leave your kiln unobserved at this point.* This is the crucial stage (1000°–1200°F) where your glass will begin to droop and set over the mold. The exact temperature and time duration will vary depending on the manufacturer and the type of glass. So it is important that you remain to watch it.

10. Take periodic *fast* glances at your glass either through the peephole or by opening the door just a crack. *Wear a protective mitten or use the kiln hood because the door will be hot.*
11. *The instant that you see your glass begin to droop over the mold, turn off the third heating element. This will reduce the heat thereby slowing down the drooping process.*

The reason that we believe that the bending must be accomplished slowly can best be explained by comparing glass bending to baking a cake: When our mothers took a straw to test the "doneness" of a cake, they were trying to see if the inside of the cake was as thoroughly cooked as the outside. If it wasn't, they let it cook 10 minutes longer and then tested it again.

This theory is the same with glass bending: until the glass has finally seated itself over the mold, the same slow cake-cooking process should be followed. Glass, like the cake, has to inwardly absorb its heat from the outside. To get the middle of the glass to be the same temperature as the outer surface, you have to give the heat a chance to penetrate to its inner parts without searing the surface.

Unless the entire piece is at the same temperature, your results will be unsatisfactory. Dull or nonexistent glazes (shine) burnt finishes, raised or depressed bubbles, and various other deformities are all caused by rushing the process, thereby creating unevenly applied heat. A very slow process will guarantee a highly polished glaze and complete conformity to the mold.

12. When you observe that the glass has uniformly seated itself on the mold and the drooping process is complete, write down the final temperature of your pyrometer, probably between 1400°–1425°F. *Immediately shut off your remaining heating elements and momentarily open the door to allow a blast of hot air to escape then close it.* This will halt the rise in temperature. If the temperature goes as little as 25° beyond the bending stage, the glass may react in a variety of negative ways as mentioned on page 129. Hopefully the slow process we have just outlined will prevent any sudden rise and allow you ample time to arrest any rise in case it does go beyond this "final" bending temperature. (See Illustration 4-3.)

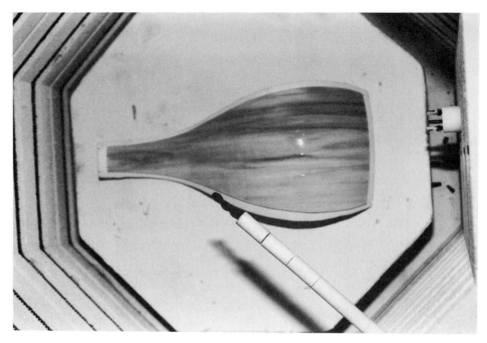

Illustration 4-3

You should now hold the kiln temperature 5–10°F below the final temperature by keeping a constant eye on the pyrometer. There will be slight temperature rises again because of the closed door and heat buildup from the firebrick around the kiln, in the shelf, and in the mold and glass themselves. Crack open the door intermittently as the temperature rises until it levels off at that 5–10° point below your final drooping temperature.

Now that you've fired your kiln and bent your glass, phase II of the process should begin: *Annealing and Cooling Off.*

Just as you patiently fired your kiln and glass, this second phase must be done slowly. By raising the temperature of and bending the glass, you have created stress points in the glass. You need to relieve these stress points to prevent the cooled-down glass from cracking. Just as a glassblower must place a blown goblet into an annealing oven in order to "fix" the glass and strengthen it, drooped glass needs to be fixed (annealed) in order to render it less brittle. Your drooped/bent glass is even more brittle than the flat glass was. To give you an idea of its brittleness, just think of what would have happened had you tried to bend the original flat glass by using your hands. The annealing process will complete the bending stage.

As mentioned previously, all glass has its own unique characteristics. Just as different types or brands will begin to bend at different temperatures, so too will it anneal at various temperatures. If you write to the manufacturer of the glass you are bending, he should give you the range at which his glass should be annealed. Roughly speaking, most glass is annealed between 950° and 1050°F.

You'll begin the annealing at the highest point of the annealing temperature:

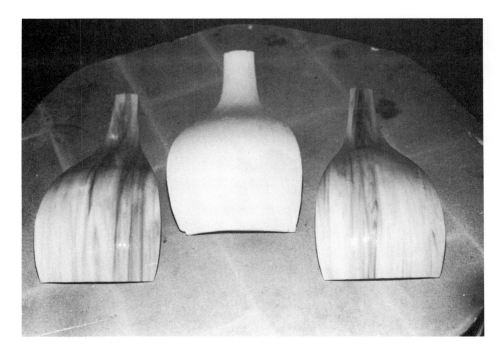

Illustration 4-4

Illustration 4-5

Illustration 4-6

ANNEALING

1. Depending on what your final temperature is after bending, manipulate your door or heating element switches until the pyrometer reads 1000°F and remains there for a period of time. It is at this high point that you will most quickly relieve the stress points.
2. Hold the temperature at 1000°F for 1½ to 2 hours by playing with the switches in the same manner for firing and drooping: turn on or off one heating element at a time while closely observing the pyrometer.
3. After annealing for the manufacturer's specified time, kill all the switches and allow the kiln and glass to cool down gradually.
4. When the glass is cooled *down to the point where you can actually pick it up with your hands,* your annealing is finished. Use the "hot iron" method of quickly touching and pulling your hand away to see if its cool enough to grasp. If the glass is so hot that you have to handle it with tongs, there is a good chance that it would fracture the minute you removed it from the kiln and it hits the "cool" air. So, *wait* until the glass is cool.

5. Now you must inspect your glass. Check its contour with the mold's; examine the glass for bubbles or imperfections; make certain whether the original bright shine is still present, dulled, or improved; and examine the edges of the glass for a consistent level and smooth widths and edges. (See Illustration 4-4.)

The proof of your glass pudding is in all of the above. This is where your stick-to-it-tiveness is put to the test: If your glass is too dull, you will have to do everything over again *but slow down the firing stage.* If your edges aren't right, you overfired through the bending stage. If there are bubbles or bumps in your glass, you cooled the glass down too fast.

This is where your notes come into play. Depending upon your problem, you will have to make appropriate adjustments on your next try. Play with the switches differently to raise or lower temperatures; adjust your time frames if necessary. But the important thing is to do it again *if you have the time.* This first bending required several hours; you will need the same relative amount for the next bending and you cannot rush time.

But once you establish temperature parameters and time frames for a specific type of glass by manufacturer, you will have established the standards for any other future bending of that brand of glass.

You might have to crack a lot of eggs along the way, but the glass omelets you will make will be well worth it. These bending standards will have to be established before you can move on to any project.

These initial steps are fun in themselves and extremely gratifying when your glass comes out right; but the finished projects, like the pictured lampshade, are even more gratifying as the sum of their parts. (See Illustrations 4-5 and 4-6.)

5

Restoration and Repair

With the exploding interest in and demand for original and new stained glass art, there has also been a corresponding demand for antique windows and lampshades of all types. However, much of the stained glass we have seen that was produced during the early part of the century is in various stages of disrepair and could use some fixing. This dual demand has created a very special area of activity for stained glass artisans who wish to take on the responsibilities of restoration. And, in fact, much of our own business over the past few years has been devoted to reconstructing dilapidated windows and cracked lampshades.

Besides this obvious need for restoration of older stained glass objects, a week rarely goes by when one of our students or a customer does not bring in a recently completed project that might have a hairline fracture in the glass, a missing piece of glass, a widening gap between lead and glass, or some other problem needing a solution. The point is that because of the fragile nature of the materials, stained glass is in many ways much like an automobile: no matter how well cared for, time, weather and unavoidable accidents necessitate occasional maintenance. And, compared to other areas of stained glass work, relatively little literature is available on repair and restoration. The occasional article or an incidental mention in other manuals generally is not detailed enough to cover the myriad problems encountered with this type of work. We hope that this chapter begins to fill the gap in this vital area of stained glass education.

While there cannot be a hard set of rules for tackling all repair or restoration projects, since each one is a unique situation, there are some general guidelines that stained glass artists can follow when approaching this type of work. For this chapter, we will take you step-by-step through the various techniques we have employed with individual repair projects while simultaneously discussing general techniques for universal application of each step. In this way we can show you from beginning to end how restoration demands individual approaches while proceeding from general guidelines.

One last *caveat:* Repair and restoration can be perhaps the most frustrating of all stained glass work. You have to be prepared for any eventuality, and the responsibility creates a pressure that is absent when beginning a project from scratch, or when you are working with totally new materials. Before beginning, you have to mentally prepare yourself for the fact that this may be very tedious and repetitious work. But once accomplished, restoration can be a most gratifying experience. To paraphrase the poet, to know that you preserved a thing of beauty that will probably outlast you is indeed a joy forever.

Approach, Evaluation, and Planning

The most obvious method of approach when confronted with any repair problem is to *proceed with patient caution.* Before you start ripping lead out and removing glass, *evaluate* what really needs to be done, why you need to do it, and how you are going to accomplish it. Do not merely concern yourself with the immediate repair area; a leaded window or lamp's structure generally depends upon the tight butting of different pieces of glass held together by a soldered piece of lead. If there is a weakness in one area, there may be others all the way down the line. Examine every other piece of glass, solder joint, and strip of lead. If there is trauma to one area, chances are that some other area has also been affected. Accidents with stained glass resemble in type a rear-end collision: one jolt can cause multiple dents, breakage, and whiplash.

While you are slowly and closely examining the entire project, jot down what you find. Indicate where it is on the object by marking it with a grease pencil or piece of tape or describing its location in your notes. The reason for this notetaking is that your next step will be to write out an engagement plan that outlines exactly what you are going to do. We feel that by putting something down on paper, it forces you to approach the repair logically and completely. It also helps you when dealing with clients and estimating costs. We cannot emphasize enough this aspect of preparation. Things are not always what they appear to be on the surface, especially when dealing with older objects. The engagement plan allows you to "see" this by analyzing the object's structure and realizing the interdependency of each piece of glass lead line and reinforcing bars.

This engagement plan will help you determine whether a panel or lamp requires minor repair or major restoration. You will need to determine this because of the important time and compensation factors (if you are working for a client). If any of us are repairing a window for our own private collection, we assume every project is a major restoration. We will spare no expense or involvement in order to return the project to its original shape and quality.

However, if you are dealing with a client, time and material factors translate to money and client-cost. Sometimes you may have to work up two engagement plans—on that will be short-term, a plug-the-hole repair, and another for a complete restoration. If a minor repair will do the job adequately, fine; but if you feel that to maintain your integrity as a stained glass artist, a major restoration involving time and money is the only option for a dilapidated panel or lamp, you must tell a client so. After explaining in detail what needs to be done, and giving a client as accurate a cost estimate as possible, it is then up to the client whether to invest the money. Do not sacrifice your standards or compromise your professional judgment to satisfy a client's reluctance to meet your fee, because if you do, chances are it will come back to haunt you.

After determining what you are going to have to do, you will have to decide where you will perform the work—on-site or in your workshop. With lamps or smaller

TOOLS AND MATERIALS

Tool/Material	Brand/Description	Available At . . .
A) FOILED LAMP		
Solder-off™, 1 roll		Hardware store/ Stained glass supply store
X-acto knife	Pointed blade	Hardware or art supply store
Patinas	Allnova®	Stained glass supply store
Two braising rods	12″ long, brass	Quality craft supply or building supply store
Rubber-tipped hammer		Tool supplier/ Hardware store
Offset needlenose pliers		Hardware store
Soldering tools		
Cutting tools		
Foil		

objects, there's usually no problem; you can merely take them down and bring them to your workshop.

Windows can be a different story, though. *It is best to always remove installed windows or panels and work with them flat on a worktable.* However, in some cases it might be impossible, or for just a one- or two-piece repair, not worth the trouble of removing a window from the sash or frame. Perhaps, also, too many pieces are cracked and removal would cause a complete collapse; or the reinforcing bars may be too solidly encased in the windowframe; or the lead has buckled too much. In short, if a window is in too fragile or permanent a state to remove, or you have only one or two minor repairs, you may have no choice but to try to do the job while the window is hanging vertically. In some cases, deciding where you will perform repairs determines the extent of your restoration.

After scrutinizing the stained glass project, making your engagement plan outlining the how's and why's of what you're going to do, and then deciding where to do the project, you should take a picture or make an exact cartoon of your entire project. You can make a cartoon by superimposing paper over the object and tracing its raised outline. You should then number each piece of glass (even the broken or missing

TOOLS AND MATERIALS

Tool/Material	Brand/Description	Available At . . .
B) LEADED WINDOW		
Wire brush	Similar to a long toothbrush	Hardware or stained glass supplier
Patinas		Stained glass supply store
Glazing compound	Sterling, black	Hardware store
Lobster pick or pointed object		
Copper wire	10-gauge	Hardware store
Various screwdrivers		
Chisel		
Nails		
Welding or concrete reinforcing bars or rods	Miscellaneous tools dependent on the restoration	
Soldering tools		
Glass-cutting tools		
Lead came		

ones) and its corresponding pattern so that if you have to rip the entire thing apart you will have a reference for putting it all back together.

All this preparatory work should be accomplished before you begin to physically do anything. Even when the repair seems to be only a simple one- or two-piece replacement, it never hurts to be sure.

Now let's get into some actual repair.

Foiled Lampshade Repair

The reason this lampshade needs repair stems from its poorly braced aperature (see Illustration 5-1) from which the shade hangs and is supported when connected to the electrical hardware and ceiling chain. The supporting crossbar, the vase cap, and the

Illustration 5-1

hardware pulled away primarily because of poor soldering of the crossbar and lack of reinforcement. It came crashing down, twenty-seven pieces were broken, and the skirt was slightly bent out of shape. We will tackle this support problem in the same manner as outlined in our section on lampshade bracing in Chapter 1 after we've taken care of the broken pieces.

Although there are many broken pieces butting each other, we are going to approach the first piece as if it were the *only* one broken. This will give you the technique for repairing odd or single broken pieces, which are a pretty common problem.

Your first concern with a foiled lamp (or panel, for that matter) should be the butting pieces: *you want to remove the broken pieces without disturbing the unbroken pieces or damaging the soldered foil on the neighboring pieces.* If you do damage either, it will only create more work for you and bring attention to the repaired area. (See Illustration 5–2.)

Keep this goal in mind as we proceed:

1. First, in order to carefully disengage the broken piece, you must remove the solder from the foiled seam that cements the broken piece to the "good" pieces. Just as your flux is important when applying solder, it is equally important in its removal. Generously flux the perimeter seams of the broken piece. Then overlay the Solder-Off™ on the seam and apply your soldering iron. The solder will adhere to your Solder-Off™ strip and its magnet-like attraction will neatly remove the solder without removing the foil. (See Illustrations 5-3, 5-4, and 5-5.) *Do not disturb or damage the foil on the "good" butting pieces.* If you directly applied your iron to the solder to remove it, gravity would pull your solder down or in different directions and it might

Illustration 5-2

Illustration 5-3

Illustration 5-4

Illustration 5-5

drop on other "good" seams, creating more problems. And you would probably damage the foil on the "good" piece, *which you want to take pains not to do.* Remove all the solder from all the bordering seams.

2. With your X-acto™ knife, *remove the foil from the broken piece only by sliding it under the foil and lifting it off.* (See Illustration 5-6.) Slide it along the perimeter to loosen the glue and free it from the glass.

3. You must now carefully disengage the splintered pieces of glass without damaging the abutting piece.* (See Illustration 5-7.)

   We first try to do this by *gently rapping* the broken pieces with the blunt end of the X-acto™ knife and pushing them through. (See Illustration 5-8.) If you cannot punch them out, you may need to make a few more scores to create smaller fractures. (See Illustration 5-9.) With these stubborn pieces, you may also have to use your offset pliers to grasp the broken piece while carefully applying heat only to its foiled borders and not its abutting pieces and slowly pulling it away. (See Illustration 5-10.)

4. Lastly, you must now remove the remaining foil from the broken piece without damaging the abutting foil. *You will need heat, patience,* and a *gentle touch.* (See Illustration 5-11.) Apply direct heat to the "damaged" foil and allow it to naturally pull away from the adjoining foil by applying very little pulling force with your offset pliers. (See Illustration 5-12.) *Take your time because this is an extremely critical point.* If you remove the abutting "good" foil, you will have to refoil or possibly replace that abutting piece.

5. After removal of the excess foil, remove any excess solder around the edges of the surrounding "good" pieces so that you have a neat, "clean" hole. (See Illustration 5-13.)

6. You must now make a custom pattern of your hole to use for cutting a replacement piece. Place a white piece of paper *behind* the hole and with a fine-tipped felt marker, trace the pattern for a new piece. (See Illustration 5-14.)

7. Cut the new replacement piece and fit it to the opening, adjusting any deviation. This piece must fit *exactly:* router, file, or recut until it fits tightly. Then, naturally, foil the entire piece. (See Illustration 5-15.)

8. Place the piece in the hole and gently tap it into place with your rubber-tipped hammer so that it is on an even level with the abutting pieces' edges. (See Illustration 5-16.)

9. Tack-solder it in place and then finish tack-soldering the entire perimeter. (See Illustrations 5-17 and 5-18.)

---

*As can be seen, an abutting piece is already broken. In some cases, you can remove the solder from both pieces and then remove the glass without worrying about damaging either. But in this case, by removing all the butting broken pieces, we could not get a "true" trace of the needed replacement pieces. Also, by removing eight or four pieces together, there is a chance of creating more structural difficulties (especially in the skirt) or weaknesses. This is why in our engagement plan we decided to begin with the body and replace piece-by-piece rather than initiate a blanket removal.

And as mentioned previously, by approaching the broken pieces (especially the first piece to be repaired) as if they were the sole damaged piece surrounded by all "good" pieces, we could describe a solution to a most common problem while presenting a technique for a larger problem.

Illustration 5-6

Illustration 5-7

Illustration 5-8

Illustration 5-9

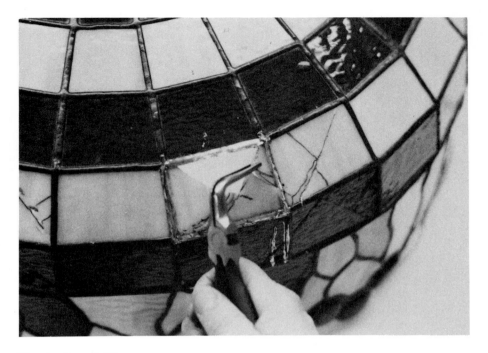

Illustration 5-10

Illustration 5-11

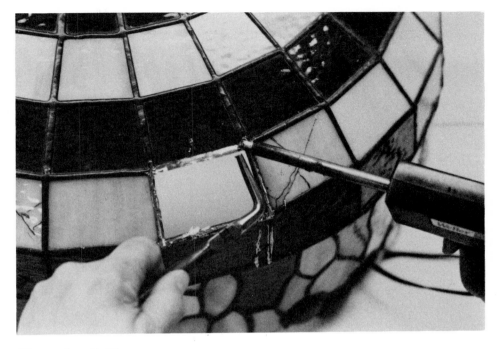

Illustration 5-12

Illustration 5-13

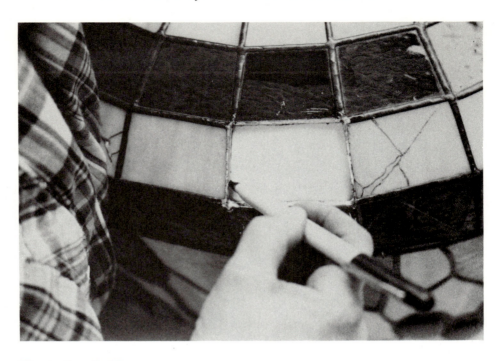

Illustration 5-14

Illustration 5-15

Illustration 5-16

Illustration 5-17

Illustration 5-18

10. You now have completely replaced one piece. We had to repeat this
procedure for all the broken pieces in the body of the lamp as shown in
Illustration 5-19. You will notice that we have not tried to raise a finished,
rounded, solder bead. This will be our final replacement step after we have
replaced every broken piece. We'll do this using our leveling method
described in Chapter 1.

Now that we have stabilized the body of the lamp, we have to attack the skirt which
absorbed the biggest shock. (See Illustration 5-20.) The major difficulty with the skirt
is the number of butting pieces that need replacement. (See Illustration 5-21.) If we do
a wholesale removal, the skirt might lose its rounded shape. Then we would need to
place the shade on an exact mold and rebuild the shade.

We chose to do a piece-by-piece removal (just like the body) because of this.
Precise care in removal of cracked pieces, foil, and solder was not such a critical issue
(except where the edge of a newly repaired piece butted a cracked one) since many
abutting pieces were going to be removed.

There was one overriding consideration: depending upon the situation, a bracing
wire was needed to prevent the separating of "good" foil from "good" pieces and,
consequently, the expansion of the skirt. This can be done by soldering a brass or
copper wire at either solder seam of a piece that might need bracing because of a
weakness created by an abutting broken piece. (See Illustration 5-22.)

This will allow removal of a broken piece without the threat of further expansion
or damage to "good" pieces while maintaining the skirt's proper and original shape.

Illustration 5-19

Illustration 5-20

Illustration 5-21

Illustration 5-22

11. After replacing all the broken pieces in the skirt, then soldering a finished solder bead around all of them, we wanted to give the skirt extra support and reinforcement. So we wrapped and soldered a strip of lead came around the entire skirt, just as we do for all our shades (Chapter 1, pp. 24 and 26). (See Illustration 5-23.)

12. Finally, and most importantly, we wanted to prevent this shade from crashing down again. As mentioned in the beginning, poor soldering of the crossbar and lack of reinforcing brazing rods in the original construction really caused the damage. The technique of soldering brazing rods is the same as outlined in Chapter 1, pp. 20–22. (See Illustration 5-24.) After shaping two of them to your lamp's seams, tinning them, and soldering them in place, completely and generously solder your crossbar to them. This should ensure that the original problem's cause will not repeat itself. (See Illustration 5-25.)

Always finish your repair work by darkening or coloring all your newly soldered seams with a patina or copper sulphate solution that will match the soldered seams of the rest of the lamp. (See Illustration 5-26.)

And don't forget to thoroughly clean the outside *as well as the inside* before reattaching any electrical hardware.

Illustration 5-23

Illustration 5-24

Illustration 5-25

Leaded Window

Repairing or restoring a leaded window requires different strategies involving, for the most part, different techniques from those for foiled lamps or windows. Also, old leaded windows are pregnant with more potential castastrophes than foiled projects because of the interlocking structure of the leaded window. We'll discuss these general properties that are present in all leaded repair as we specifically deal with our example window.

Keep in mind, however, that each restoration project has its unique problems. And they and their solutions must be analyzed before doing any specific work.

TOOLS AND MATERIALS

Besides your inventory of *soldering* and *cutting* tools and materials you'll need:

Darkening Patina.   You cannot have black (old) and silver (new) lead interwined: the new lead must match the old lead for authenticity.

Wire Brush.   As a result of years of oxidation to the lead, which gives it its black color but simultaneously "coats" the lead, it is necessary to scrape off this built-up oxidation (as well as dirt or grime) in order to solder new joints where old and new lead meet.

Lead Came.   Make sure you match the same width and channel depth of the new to the old.

Lobster Pick or Pointed Dowel.   You will need to remove the plaster of Paris-based cement from the lead channels in order to fit the new glass. Any small sharp-pointed object will work. Exercise care when cleaning out the channels so as not to damage the malleable and impressionable lead.

Sterling Glazing Compound (Black). After reconstructing the window, the new lead sections and some of the old may have to be cemented in order to cushion the glass and give the window extra body. The Sterling glazing compound is better and faster to use than any plaster of Paris/linseed oil formula. Also, it will not harden, disintegrate, and fall out as the years go by.

You may also need wood chisels, screwdrivers, nails, reinforcing bars (we use concrete reinforcing bars) copper wire and nails; and a hammer, depending on the project, to help you extricate or replace a window in a frame or sash.

METHODS

Of course, you should follow our evaluation guidelines, pp. 131–133, before you begin to rip anything apart. After going through our checklists, we saw that time, nature, and pollutants have made the lead expand and contract many times over, contributing to disintegration around the edges; much of the plaster of Paris cement has fragmented and fallen out; the initial trauma as well as natural stresses have caused solder joints to split; and, while most of the glass has remained in the panel, the missing pieces and cracks in other pieces sustained in the initial trauma have contributed to a slight buckling and structural weakening of the panel. (See Illustrations 5-27 and 5-28.)

Besides these technical aspects of the restoration, an important aesthetic problem for this (as well as all repairs) had to be considered: the type and color of the glass/holes that need replacement. The chances of exactly matching new glass to the old in texture and color are generally slim and in many cases impossible. (In fact, we have had to glue impossible-to-replace glass together in order to restore some windows.) Sometimes you must settle for replacement glass that is the least different from the other glass, viewed from a back-lighted and unlighted perspective. And, at times, you may have to remove "good" or unbroken pieces of old glass and replace them with new glass in order to restore a window that does not look like a patchwork quilt of new and old glass when finished.

The problem with this window's glass was the deep cobalt-blue color as well as the painted design fired on the broken pieces (and most of the other glass). Because of time

Illustration 5-26

Illustration 5-27

and cost factors involved with painting and firing, and the client's wishes, we decided to redistribute the unbroken inner border pieces and cut new, unpainted frosted glass (which appears to be "old") to create the outer border.

After determining all this *before* we started any physical work, it was time to begin:

1. The first thing to do was to *extricate the window from the frame.* This is generally no easy task. In many cases, putty around the edges is extremely difficult to remove because of the near petrification of the putty. A hammer and chisel is sometimes needed to scrape it down. And, needless to say, working with a hammer and chisel around the borders of a window requires meticulous care. In addition, you never know what's going to happen to the window when the constriction of the frame is removed and the window "expands." In many cases, there is a reverse chain-reaction when the anchor nails are taken out and the panel is "sprung."

Luckily none of the above happened with this window. Since the border was shot, we merely had to cut the occasional lead strips connecting the rest of the panel to the frame as *it was lying flat.*

Illustration 5-28

2. To avoid making the panel larger than it was originally, it is always best to trace the perimeter of your frame opening, then construct a border with ¼-inch molding around the pattern. This should guarantee that your panel will fit back into the frame, even allowing for a warped frame.

3. Most leaded windows have reinforcing bars soldered to their backs for support, as did this one. Removal of the reinforcing bar facilitates the repair and allows the panel to lie flat.

4. If a window has buckled, as this one has slightly, there are a couple of approaches you can take to correct it. *Don't ever push down on it to flatten it as you would a jack-in-the-box.* The sudden stress could fracture many pieces. If *slightly* buckled, you can expose the buckled area to gentle heat from a quartz heater, sun, or ultraviolet lamp, and gingerly and distributively pat it down, a little as a time, as the lead warms.

For severe buckling, the only method that will cure it is a complete ripout of the lead and glass in a broadcast pattern from the buckled area to the border, and a reconstruction with new materials. Since a leaded window's structure and stability depend upon the tight butting of numerous pieces of glass, held together by a supporting and equally tight strip of lead, this is the only method that will ensure a tight window free from buckling or lead spaces.

5. Since exact replacement of the painted cobalt inner border pieces was impractical, we decided that we would retain the four good pieces opposite each other in pairs as one border and construct a "new" border on the other two adjacent sides. We would retain the small painted cubes as originally placed since none were broken.

In order to accomplish the above, we had to remove all the damaged lead and carefully pull out the "good" pieces we were going to retain. When doing this, you can cut away butting lead, but it becomes necessary to burn away each old joint in order to open up the channel so that a custom-cut replacement will fit exactly.

You must also scrape out all the old cement or putty with your lobster pick or sharp object from any lead channels so that you will have a wide-open gap for the glass. (When you remove any "old" glass that is to be retained, it may have cement stuck to it. You must remove this cement by soaking the pieces in a solution of warm water and ammonia long enough for the cement to soften and be removed easily with a razorblade.)

6. Now we needed to tighten up the window by pushing the glass and lead inward toward the center and bracing it against the molding (temporarily). We scrutinized the panel for split solder joints that required resoldering. You have to scrape each joint with a wire brush to remove the grime and oxidation from the solder and lead came. When the joint and lead are silver, flux generously, and then solder while pinching or pushing the lead and glass together with your free hand. Go over the entire panel when performing this process. When completed, this resoldering of joints will be an important contribution to the structural strengthening of any panel that needs restoration.

7. The cutting of custom replacement pieces for this panel wasn't difficult since they were all border pieces and we had an old piece from which to draw an exact pattern. And the outer border was merely a long strip whose width was the difference between the frame molding we constructed and the rest of the panel. However, if you had to replace a piece within the panel somewhere near the center, you would place a white sheet of paper *under* the hole (after removing any broken glass and putty) and trace a custom pattern (see our lampshade repair section, p. 137). The difficult part in this situation is the placing of the new piece into the gap that is surrounded by the channeled lead. The top of the came is an obstacle to your snapping it in. And you cannot cut the glass any smaller because it would not fit into the grooves and fall right through. You have to *carefully* lift the edge of the top lead channel of one side by grasping it with the teeth of a Fletcher cutter and slightly bending it back (up) to allow you to slide the replacement glass in. Since you do not want to create too many deep teeth marks in the soft lead, this is a procedure that requires a great deal of care and should be slowgoing.

After you get the glass in, you must press the lead back down by applying even and level pressure over the length of the lead with a straightedge or another tool that will accomplish this task. Since the lead is impressionable, if you randomly or unevenly press it back down, you may create tiny and noticeable wrinkles in the lead.

8. After all your old and broken pieces of glass and lead are replaced and your lead and old joints are soldered on one side, you must naturally turn the panel over and solder all the appropriate joints on the back. Use your wire brush at any joint where old meets new lead or where an old joint has split.

9. While the panel is on its back, you should begin the cementing process, which will cushion the glass against the lead and seal any gaps. This involves the forcing of your Dap glazing compound between the lead and glass at the restored areas, and then removing any excess putty. This technique is similar to glazing normal windowglass in that you apply a generous amount of putty, forcing it under the lead, and passing a putting knife or small, flat screwdriver over it while pushing it inward.

10. After the back is cemented, turn the panel over and cement the front side.

11. After cementing the front, a thorough cleaning with warm water and

ammonia should take place. For some silly reason, primarily born out of ignorance or snobbishness, many people think an "antique" window has to be filthy to reflect its authenticity. We feel that a rigorous cleaning, rather than destroying its value, will enhance its beauty and appreciate its value.

12. The cleaning will make the next step less complicated and difficult. We call it "creative chemistry." You must apply a darkening agent or patina to the new lead in order to match the old lead's oxidation. This is a matter of trying one or a combination of various patinas (or acids) that are presently available at stained glass suppliers. If you cannot get the new lead dark enough after repeated applications, wait a few hours and reapply.

13. You must turn the panel over once again (to the back) and clean the glass and darken the lead. You must also replace the reinforcing bar if, as in our case, you removed it.

It is generally wise to replace the old copper wire that is soldered to the panel and holding the bar (with some windows you may have to add bars, also.) Proceed as follows:

    a. Cut 1½-inch strips of medium-gauge copper wire.
    b. Melt away the old solder and scrape the lead where the copper wire will be attached.
    c. Lay the copper strips flat on the lead, *flux* the center of the wire and the lead, and *solder* the wire at its center to the lead.
    d. Place the reinforcing bar on top of the flattened wire and tightly twist the wire three or four times around the bar with pliers. (See Illustration 5-29.) As you twist, you will feel and almost see the glass and lead tighten up and become more rigid and sturdy.
    e. Finish by cutting off the excess tips of the wire down to the twist. (See Illustration 5-30.)

14. Your final job, as was ours, is the replacement of the window in the sash or frame. Sometimes this is not an easy task, but if your frame molding was accurate, and the sash has not shifted or warped, you should have no problem. Carefully place the window in the frame, replace any holding nails, and neatly glaze (putty) the window, if necessary. (See Illustrations 5-31 and 5-32.)

Summary

Most of the techniques outlined for repairing foiled lampshades are applicable to any foiled project, including panels; and the same is true for leaded panels and lampshades. In addition, many techniques are common to both methods of assembly. You will find that you will experiment with these methods (and various tools when the unique restoration requires it) regardless of the medium. Since much of restoration work is an exercise of your "glass sense" and application of your skill, experience, and repair strategies, you'll be able to "see" what it needs as you evaluate each specific job.

And that is what we would like to underline once again: Each restoration and repair is uniquely different. Your assessment of what is needed is driven by many

Illustration 5-29

Illustration 5-30

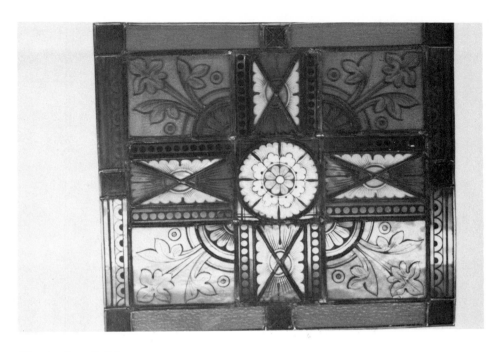

Illustration 5-31

Illustration 5-32

factors—physical, aesthetic, financial, and, in some cases, business. All the general and specific methods and strategies presented here will assist you when you take on the responsibility or task when repairing an original work of art. But, because of the nature of the work, none of our repair guidelines should be considered absolute nor all-encompassing.

Another point we would like to re-emphasize is the unpredictability of a restoration project. Sometimes your methodical and deliberate plans and guesstimates will need revising; and many times, your goals will not be realized. You cannot become frustrated or anxious when things are not conforming to your engagement plan. You will have to constantly step back, take a break, re-evaluate, and adjust as you go along.

The above is especially true in regard to time. If you are repairing something for yourself, do not set any target dates. If someone approaches you to do a repair, and wants to know how much it will cost and how long it will take, avoid giving estimates carved in concrete. We have learned from sad experience that nothing except quality of workmanship should be guaranteed. Estimating time and labor costs is a gamble when dealing with an unscientific activity such as restoration. You cannot afford to rush a project or take short cuts in order to make a target date or fall within a profitable time frame in regard to price.

Finally, we do not want to deceive you into believing that repair is the easiest, hassle-free stained glass operation. It is precisely because of its plodding difficulty, and at times, boring, tedious little jobs, coupled with the knowledge that you are not creating your own original work, that makes many people refuse to get involved with restoration.

But, we believe that the urgent need for preserving such beautiful objects of art, the challenges present, the special skills involved, and the satisfaction we feel looking at a project "after" when we knew its imperfect condition "before," all make restoration and repair worth the cost and time.

Appendix

A Note on Stained Glass Suppliers

Any kind of "comprehensive" list of stained glass suppliers would probably be incomplete, inaccurate, and exclusionary by the time you buy and read this book.

If you've bought this book from a stained glass supplier, you should not have a problem purchasing everything you need to accomplish all our tasks and projects. If you acquire our book at a local bookstore, and you really do not know where to go, you can do one of the following:

1. Check the Yellow Pages of your local telephone directories under "Glass—Leaded" or "Glass—Stained." They should provide enough leads. (You can also visit a public library and peruse the Yellow Pages of a large city directory and call or write for their catalog.)
2. You can write or call local, regional, or state art councils or associations for a list of their members. Some of them may deal in stained glass supplies.
3. Or, you can send a self-addressed, stamped, legal-sized envelope and $3.00 to us—Mt. Tom Studio, 58 Strong Street, Easthampton, MA 01027; and we will send out our regional and countrywide list of suppliers and mail-order houses that will satisfy your stained glass requirements.

Glossary

Anneal The hardening of glass (after heating or scoring) which renders the glass less brittle.

Blind soldering Our method of soldering a piece of glass onto the back of a host piece by drilling a hole through the host glass, applying a brass pin to the piece to be attached, and foiling and soldering the pin to the back of the host glass.

Brazing rod A thin brass rod used to reinforce stained glass projects.

Flat-solder The soldering of a project which raises no rounded bead but rather lies flat on the foiled seam.

Greenware A kiln-fired piece of molded ceramic slip or plaster of Paris.

Router A grinding/filing machine for eliminating excess glass after an imprecise score.

Tack-solder An incomplete method of soldering a project together with "globs" of solder at intervals that temporarily solidifies its structure for a final, finished soldering bead.

Tinning The presoldering of wrapped pieces of glass or pieces of metal (e.g., brazing rods, crossbars) in order to facilitate their adherence to a host piece of glass or metal.

Index

Allnova™ (patina), 6, 26
Aluminum Foil, 42
Annealing, 126–129, 159

Blind Soldering, 49–77, 159
    Tools and Materials for, 49–50
Brasso ®, 26
Butterfly Mirror Project, 55–61

Caged Parrot Project, 78–87
Canopy Terrarium, 87–102
Cartoon, 132
Clockworks (quartz), 102, 114, 118
Conical Point Soldering Tip, 56
Copper Sulphate, 147
Crossbar Attachment, 22–23

Diamond Bits, 49, 53–54

Elmer's Glue, 29
Engagement Plan for Repair, 131

Fletcher Glass Cutter, 153
Floral Clock Project, 102–118

Getting Started in Stained Glass, ix
Glastar Router, 49, 50, 53, 67
Glass
    Bent, 119–129
    Blank of, 124
    Draping, 121–122
    Sagging, 121–122
Glass Pro™ Silver Protector, 7, 59, 114
Glass Wax, 26
"Glob" Soldering Method, 13, 19, 46
Glossary, 159
Greenware, 123, 159

Kerosene, 52
Kiln, 119–121

Lampshades, 1–48
    Flat Paneled, 1–26
        Assembly, 10–19
        Blocking Board for, 8
        Bracing, 20–22
        Crossbar for, 22–23

Cutting out, 7–10
Finishing Touches, 24–26
Patterns, 2–5
Soldering, 13, 19, 46
Tools, 6
Iris (molded), 26–48
    Assembly, 44–66
    Bracing, 46
    Cutting and Fitting, 35–37
    Design Transferral, 29–35
    Foiling, 37–40
    Mold for, 28–29
    Soldering, 42–44
Leveling Method of Soldering, 19

Mercury, 77
Mt. Tom Stained Glass Artists, ix
Mt. Tom Studio, 158
Mt. Tom Train Project, 55, 61–77

Oxidation, 41, 153, 154

Plaster-of-Paris, 122–123
    Pushpins, 11, 95
    Pyrometer, 120, 121, 124

Razorblade, 24
Reinforcing Bars, 148, 154
Restoration and Repair, 130–157

Solder-Off™, 132, 134
Spackle, 29
Stained Glass Supplies, 158
Steel Wool, 44
Sterling Glazing Compound, 133, 148

Tack Soldering, 13, 39, 159
Three-Dimensional Projects, 78–118
Tinning, 22, 46, 159
Two-Way Tape, 30, 36

U Came, 24, 101

Vase Cap, 46–47

Worden Molds, 29

X-acto Knife, 137